THE

DORSET

YEAR BOOK

FOR 2014

ONE HUNDRED AND FIFTH YEAR OF ISSUE

First published in Great Britain in 2013 by The Society of Dorset Men

A CIP catalogue record for this book is available from the British Library.

Paperback ISBN 978-0-9926594-0-0
Price £6.00

Edited by Trevor Vacher-Dean

Printed and bound in Great Britain by
Print Team (Dorset) Limited
www.printteam.co.uk

Our Cover: Four Memorials where "Dorset remembers its war dead"
Main picture: Abbotsbury with, from the top, Fontmell Magna, Dorchester
and Swanage. Pictures by Year Book Photographer, Shaun Cregan.

CONTENTS

THE SOCIETY OF DORSET MEN

FOUNDED JULY 7th, 1904

'A Silver Tower Dorset Red Banner Bears'

President:
LORD FELLOWES OF WEST STAFFORD, DL

Deputy Presidents:
SIR ANTHONY JOLLIFFE, GBE, DL, D.Sc, D.Mus
JEREMY POPE, OBE, DL
JAMES WELD, DL

Hon. Deputy President:
GORDON E. HINE, FRICS
ROY ADAM, MBE

Past Presidents:
SIR FREDERICK TREVES, BART, GCVO, CB, LLD, 1904 - 1907
THOMAS HARDY, OM, LITT.D, JP, 1907 - 1909
COLONEL JOHN MOUNT BATTEN, CB, 1909 - 1911
COLONEL SIR ROBERT WILLIAMS, BART, VD, 1911 - 1913
SIR STEPHEN COLLINS, JP, 1913 - 1915
JOHN CASTLEMAN SWINBURNE-HANHAM, JP, 1915 - 1919
THE RIGHT HON. The EARL of SHAFTESBURY, KP, PC, GCVO, 1919 - 1922, 1924 - 1925
CAPTAIN THE RIGHT HON. F. E. GUEST, CBE, DSO, 1922 - 1924
CAPTAIN ANGUS V. HAMBRO, DL, JP, 1925-33, 1936 - 1944
LIEUT.-COL. SIR PHILIP COLFOX, BART, MC, 1933 - 1936
H.E. THE RIGHT HON. LORD LLEWELLIN, CBE, MC, TD, DL, 1944 - 1957
BRIGADIER G. M. B. PORTMAN, CB, TD, DL, 1957 - 1961
ROBERT TOM WARREN, 1962 - 1963
COLONEL SIR RICHARD GLYN, BART, OBE, TD, DL, 1964 - 1969
SIMON WINGFIELD DIGBY, MA, TD, DL, 1970 - 1984
SIR ANTHONY JOLLIFFE, GBE, DL, D.Sc, D.Mus, 1984 - 2011

Past Hon. Secretaries:	*Past Hon. Editors:*
WILLIAM WATKINS, JP, 1904 - 1925	SIR NEWMAN FLOWER, 1914 - 1920
H. LL. WATKINS, 1925 - 1937	STANLEY L. GALPIN, 1920 - 1932
S . H. J. DUNN, 1937 - 1940	H. LL. WATKINS, 1935 - 1937
E. G. GALE, 1940 - 1941	ASHLEY C. ROGERS, 1937 - 1950
HARRY J. HARVEY, 1941 - 1942	FRANK C. H. DENNETT, 1951 - 1960
F. C. H. DENNETT, AACCA, FRES, 1942 - 1961	N. J. ('NAT') BYLES, 1961 - 1978
W. T. G. PERROTT, MIWO, 1961 - 1969	FRED LANGFORD, 1979 - 1994
J. C. R. PREWER, 1969 - 1979	GEORGE LANNING, 1995 - 2000
G. E. HINE, FRICS, 1979 - 2004	PETER PITMAN, 2001 - 2013

LETTER FROM THE EDITOR

Dear Readers,

This year is likely to be dominated by memories of conflict, being the centenary of the commencement of the 1914-18 "Great War". The Society of Dorset Men would be failing if proper acknowledgement were not given to this; hence our cover pictures and various articles throughout the publication, which are produced as a tribute to "The Fallen".

I hope that you are also presented with a Year Book that informs, enlightens, entertains and amuses with varying subject matter from all parts of the County, produced on various levels from the humorous to the scholarly and providing much of interest to you all.

Still unapologetically produced along nostalgic lines of "fostering love of County and pride in its history and traditions", I would nonetheless be pleased, for future editions, to receive articles on 'modern Dorset' and its future; on rural affairs and industry, on health matters, sport, hobbies and pastimes, music as well as art and literature, transport and all things locally interesting, to stimulate and encourage the young as well as the old. Your views on this will be welcome as *"things do change as years do vlee."*

This, my first year as Editor, has proved something of a learning curve particularly as a technological dinosaur, quite happy to use a trusty fountain pen as my main tool of communication, I knew I was in practical terms unprepared for my new role. My ability to use a computer has improved through necessity and a great deal of help. Although far from enjoying a love affair with my PC, I feel confident in advising all those who think it *daunting* to "Go for it!" Don't miss out – believe me, the rewards of computer literacy are amazing!

I would like to thank individually all who have encouraged and helped me through this exceedingly busy year, but space forbids. Suffice to say, you know who you are so please accept my heartfelt appreciation for your kindness. And to our wonderful contributors who are collectively responsible for the content of the Year Book, I offer my sincere thanks and a request (to just the odd few when they next send me copy) to pay the correct postage and thereby save me a trek to the town centre Royal Mail sorting office and the cost of the balance due plus a handling charge.

We all owe a debt of gratitude to Peter and Jill Pitman for their unremitting work as a partnership editing the Year Book over the past twelve years....so *"THANK YOU"* *Peter and Jill.*

I cannot sign off without acknowledging the role of Alex Smith, a director of Print Team and responsible for the printing of The Year Book. Without his tireless efforts and support, way above the 'call of duty', I am sure this 2014 Dorset Year Book would be considerably less than it is. I hope you all enjoy it.

Yours very sincerely

Trevor Vacher-Dean

The Whitehall Cenotaph

The Society of Dorset Men remembers

IN this centenary year, marking the start of the First World War, the Society of Dorset Men pays homage to "the fallen" with their Dorset Year Book cover, the story of the Whitehall Cenotaph and other articles.

"The most famous piece of Portland stone in the world is the Cenotaph, and it is good to see the quarry from which it came has been filled up and is now a garden." - so wrote Arthur Mee in the 1939 Dorset volume of "The King's England" series.

The great Sir Edwin Landseer LUTYENS (1869-1944) was its architect, and he wanted the purest white stone from Portland.

This meant the removal and disposal of the 'top rubble' – up to sixty feet of younger strata, including fossil soils and fossilised trees – in order to reach the valuable *WHITBED* freestone beneath the roach bed. The Whitehall Cenotaph is, as they say in the trade, a block job; the joints of the masonry no more than a sixteenth of an inch thick and a feat of great masoncraft.

The stone was extracted from a site close to Wakeham where the old parsonage house, destroyed by Oliver Cromwell, once stood. In 1919 the quarry was owned by Henry Sansom and, as early as 1924 was earthed over and made into allotments.

Although the design for the Cenotaph was sketched in "less than ten minutes" by Lutyens, praise for his work was unstinting: "the work of a genius", "inspired" and "a consummate work of art, embodying ...the poet's intuition, the mystic's creed, the great architect's mastery of subtleties of his craft..." His acclamation, it was said, was instantaneous.

The weight of the Cenotaph is approximately one-hundred-and-twenty tons. Height, thirty-five feet, base fifteen feet by eight-six, the top eleven-feet-six by six-six. The laurel wreaths, designed by Professor Derwent ARA, at the end are five feet in diameter, the one at the top, three-six. All letters and Roman numerals are approximately five inches square. It was erected in 1920.

The universal carnage of the 1914-18 war caused ten million European and Asiatic deaths, with thirty million missing or wounded. America suffered eight-hundred-thousand losses.

Bob Wollage eloquently sums up prevailing sentiments with the following poem, which he dedicated in 2000 not only to all those soldiers who lost their lives but also to the quarry crew of Portlanders (Bartholomew Hinde, Edward Hinde, Tom Simmons and Walt Slade) who worked the stone to build the Cenotaph.

CENOTAPH THOUGHTS

I sat benumbed and watched,
Emotions choked and stirred,
Tears flowing from my eyes –
My aching soul was purged.

They marched so proud – erect-
and held within their breast –
the comrades that they knew –
gone to eternal rest.

They were as one with them,
That soared on flying wind,
the years had not curtailed
man's shameful scar of sin.

They died that we might live –
To carry on the fight,
against the power of Greed –
and Self, and Darkened Night.

But then in many lands was seen –
the Rock of Portland "Hallowed" –
in sweat and blood, we gave the world
a lesson to be followed.

"Create and Build – love, sing and pray,
Bewildered Man – must find this Way."

Bibliography: Arthur Mee's DORSET – Hodder and Stoughton - 1939. David Pushman – Precious Stone of Dorset – Dorset Publishing Co. – 1987. Tom Williamson – Inigo's Stones – Matador – 2012. Bob Wollage – Cenotaph Thoughts – The Dorset Year Book 2000.

Hopalong Saturdays Stale Cakes and Jam

Peter St. John Tubbs remembers

A novelty Hop-along wrist watch

WE were three brothers, Bournemouth born. I was the eldest and our Saturday routine was to catch a bus to the Moderne Cinema in Moordown. Entrance to the Flicks was a matter of pennies and we had money enough to purchase a bag each of Tiger Nuts. These were not quite digestible but nevertheless a treat. For our money we were treated to two films; a cartoon followed by the main one starring "Hop-along Cassidy". That name speaks volumes.

Hoppy had a side-kick who always made coffee from the same beans they both ate for lunch. Of course he was included to help with the dialogue, otherwise Hoppy would have had to talk to his horse. I must add that Hoppy was never seen to hop nor was he seen to kick.

The story lines, such as they were, would entail helping the genocide of the indigenous people, known as Redskins or Red Indians. Since the films were in monochrome we none of us questioned the colour of their skins, nor that they were Indians living in America. This exercise was enacted by Hoppy's use of his six- guns. He only ever used two of these and was never seen to reload in spite of the number of Indians he managed to shoot. I remember the latter to be very noisy and could never understand their girly tribal names; Sue, Shy Ann and Cherry Key to name but a few. When they lost the battle, which they always did, they always wanted Hoppy to take up smoking by offering him their peace pipe.

Later on in life I was given for Christmas, you've guessed it, a Hop-along Cassidy wrist watch. It's still buried somewhere in the garden. Today it would probably be a collector's piece. I cannot think why?

Sausages, Gaslight and "In Town Tonight"

After the film, it was off to Grandma's for sausage and mash with Daddies sauce. Nothing was ever left on the plates or in the sauce bottle. The latter was not allowed in our own home since it was deemed 'common'...we had standards!

Come 5.20pm we were sent to the Newsagents to purchase Grandma five

Daddies favourite sauce

'Woodbines', then next door to the cake shop. There we requested three cakes. We never understood why we were often given nearer a dozen. Could it have anything to do with five thirty being closing time? Unsold cakes would, of course, be thrown in the bin today rather than given away to local kids.

Tea started with fresh bread and chunky strawberry jam. We would hook out all the strawberries leaving Grandma with just strawberry jelly, completely devoid of fruit. Did she care? She told us she had developed a taste for what was left after her boys had been at the jam pot. Bless...

Around six thirty my brothers would be sent up the wooden hill to bed. Starched bed sheets with a wool wrapped heated brick to warm them.

I was allowed to listen to the Wireless, now known as a radio, which was battery operated. Out of its speaker would come "Once again we stop the mighty roar of London's traffic to bring you "In Town Tonight". Film Stars and such like would be interviewed. Intelligent, interesting and often witty conversation was the order of the day. How times have changed!

The only time we saw Grandma rattled was when the 'Men' were in, changing her gas lighting to electricity. Her comment: "I can't understand the need. We see alright with what we have and, anyway, it will never catch on".

The Shaftesbury Bonfire Carnival

by Jack Sweet

THE evening of Monday 7th November 1898 was dry and cold. Just right for the Shaftesbury Bonfire Carnival procession, and to quote The Western Gazette, "happily dark, so the illuminating effect of the torches and lamps carried in the procession was all the more marked."

Gold Hill, Shaftesbury about 1900 from a pencil sketch by Charles G Harper

The choice of the seventh rather than the traditional 'Fifth of November' was further explained, "The celebration this year was fixed for the evening of the seventh, the Fifth falling on a Saturday, which day is not the most suitable in any town for street processions and a modest kind of revelry by night." Presumably Saturday nights were reserved for revelry of a less modest kind at the end of the working week and then back to work on Monday with little cash left to refuel such revelry!

The Carnival was under the patronage of the Mayor Councillor Norton, Alderman Wilkinson and Councillors Carpenter, Forrester and Burbridge and Mr. J. Grayson Smith; the organizing committee of 20 worthies was chaired by Mr. R. W. Borley. Funding for the revelry was a mixture of subscriptions and collections on the night with any deficit covered by the patrons and members of the committee.

The Carnival Procession assembled in the town cattle yard, and *The Western Gazette* reported that "The Committee had engaged some 60 lads to carry torches and all 33 cars* were more or less brilliantly lit up with lanterns and lamps. Masqueraders were numerous".

Once formed up, torches, lanterns and lamps lit, the procession set off led by the Shaftesbury Town Band "attired in grotesque uniforms befitting the occasion". Behind the Band came the Chairman's Carriage in which "Mr. Borley sat resplendent in the wig and gown of a Judge, accompanied by his vice-chairman and the secretary dressed as French Gentlemen and Mr. Tom Pinney playing the part of the "now dead – now alive – and doubtless much-sat-upon personage, the Emperor of China".

Then came decorated and illuminated bicycles for which prizes of ten shillings, seven and sixpence, and five shillings were given for the three best decorated machines.

Hero Cpl. Samuel Vickery VC – the Dorset Regiment

In the wake of the bicycles and accompanied with loud cheers came a car with the theme 'Heroes of the Day'. There stood Sir Herbert Kitchener, the victor of the Battle of Omdurman fought two months before on 2nd September, "who was by no means caricatured by Mr. W. Woodford" and Mr. Leslie St. Maur as Piper Findlater and Mr. F. Roper as Corporal Vickery, both winners of the Victoria Cross. Piper George Findlater of the 2nd Battalion Gordon Highlanders and Somerset born Corporal Samuel Vickery of the 1st Battalion Dorset Regiment had both won the ultimate award for gallantry in the attack on the Heights of Dargai on 20 October 1897 during the Tirah Campaign in the North West Frontier War.

A model of the Town Hall and Town Clock came next, followed by a car depicting the recent visit of an unnamed army unit and the troops' "attention to the fairer sex" which was greeted *with* cheers and laughter as was the car carrying the "New Woman" with "a Lord of Creation paying attention to an Emancipated Being". Other cars depicted comic as well as topical themes. "You Dirty Boy" starred an industrious and impatient old woman dealing with a boy with dirty ears and topical were the "mysterious cases of dog poisoning" which had lately occurred in the neighbourhood. A foretaste of 'things to come' were the 'motor-car' exhibited by Messrs Baker & Sons and Farris's Bell View Iron Works' display "lighted by electricity". Central to the procession was a nine foot high "Guido Fawkes" made by Mr. A. Willmott and the place of honour at the rear was the "Goodnight" car with a happy married couple going to bed.

The Western Gazette reported that confetti was sold along the route. People pelted one another with the many coloured adhesive bits of paper till their arms were tired and "till recognition was almost out of the question".

The procession returned to the cattle yard and the Shaftesbury Bonfire Carnival of 1898 finished with a firework display followed by band music and dancing on The Common. The *Gazette* concluded, with a hint of relief, that "Altogether, Shaftesbury spent an interesting, lively night and, happily, there were no accidents".

Cheers, peacock feathers and bags of confetti

I was intrigued by the throwing of confetti, and the following extract is from a report in *The Western Gazette* of the New Year's Eve revels in London, celebrating the end of 1899 and welcoming in the new century: "...The enthusiasm of the crowd – mostly Scotsmen – was genuine enough, but its modes of expression were limited. There were cheers, and peacock feathers, and bags of confetti." But that was all. It was a new kind of confetti, packed in oval shaped bags of gaily coloured paper attached to short sticks. You hit the man nearest to you with the bag, which burst. If he looked cross you held out your hand and brushed the confetti from his shoulders. In most cases the person attacked retaliated with more confetti, and the street sellers did a splendid trade. No-one knew why people wanted to buy peacocks' feathers but the supply was large.

Shaftesbury in November

Shaftesbury in November

* Ogilvie's 19th century "IMPERIAL DICTIONARY of the ENGLISH LANGUAGE" defines a CAR as any vehicle of dignity, solemnity or splendour. – Editor

THE SOCIETY OF DORSET MEN

At the dawn of the twentieth century
our men did go to London you see
seeking jobs which were hard to find
in dear old Dorset, left behind.

But the truth was 'twas a lonely place
jobs were scarce, and no friendly face.
Some Dorset worthies then made a plan
to help and support their fellow man.

To form a Society would be ideal
and so they did with a special meal
the Prince of Wales wished them success
which Frederick Treves read in the address.

Nowadays the reply to our gracious Queen
is written in dialect, and can be seen
as a direct link to King Alfred's reign
Our dialect was spoken in his domain.

Another thing from days of yore
The Society's emblem from Agincourt
a coat of arms in a silver tower
signifies Dorset's modest power.

The Dorset Year Book meant so much
to those in London, it kept them in touch,
and is enjoyed as much today,
as is the annual dinner; enjoyed by us men.

They men of foresight paved the way
for all that we enjoy today.
Sing praises now and celebrate
all that makes our Society great.

So raise your glasses gentlemen please
to our past and present worthies
Let's sing Hardy's motto often heard
Let's sing it proudly, "Who's A-fear'd?"

by Devina Symes

Concerning the Perils of the Sea

by Tony Bugler

ON an afternoon in the Autumn of 1954 a magnificent 75 ft. YAWL* had run into bad weather in the English Channel having set sail from The Solent en route to America. One of the crew had been swept overboard and badly hurt. The boat had put into Weymouth and the injured man taken to hospital.

Whilst walking along Weymouth harbourside I met "Doc" Wallace, the local Medical Officer of Health, who introduced me to the boat owner, Mr. Joe Louis of the Chicago Yacht Club. I was subsequently invited to replace the injured crewman to go as far as Vigo in Spain where another American would take over.

I had been filming out in Weymouth Bay with Richard Attenborough, George Baker, Bill Owen, and two Motor Torpedo Boats. It was George who, the next day, persuaded me to go.

FIONA was of wooden construction with canvas sails – no synthetic nonsense in those days. She had been built by Fife of Scotland for Sir Miles Thomas, Chairman of BOAC, and sold to Joe Louis for £30,000, who explained it was cheaper to pay the crew's expenses and buy a boat over here than to get a craft of similar quality in the United States where prices were extremely high.

Sailing with the grace of a dolphin

After obtaining a weather forecast from the Admiralty at Portland – sou'westerly 3-4 – we set sail. We were six in number, four Americans, an Oxford undergraduate and me. What an experience. I had not sailed on such a large vessel before or since. She slid through the sea with the grace of a dolphin.

Everything about the boat was giant size, including the sails and rigging. The main sheet was a very thick rope, and the main boom was the size of a telegraph pole. The ship's wheel incorporated a wooden saddle which one sat astride while steering, quite a good arrangement. The roomy dog-house on deck contained two full length bunk cushions. What glorious sailing. White sails against the blue sky.

However, the further we went down the Channel the more the wind got up and we had to shorten sail. Force six, Force seven, eight and then Force nine! I had never encountered such large waves before, boosted no doubt by the Atlantic swell. One minute we seemed to be perched on top of a ridge of hills looking down into a deep valley, and the next minute we were at the bottom of the valley looking up at the high ridge of dark water. The boat, which seemed so large in Weymouth Harbour, now seemed so tiny, but she rode along with the confidence of a small seabird.

The weather closed in, visibility was blotted out and conditions became very wild. Skipper and crew went below for refreshment, leaving me as watchman in the doghouse keeping an eye on the helmsman.

Shielded from the outer storm, I heard a loud crack and, looking up through the glass of the doghouse, saw the main boom had snapped in two about five feet from the mast. This great boom, still attached to the mainsail by rope and wire rigging, was now sashaying dangerously above the deck, threatening to break loose at any moment and come crashing down on the boat. It was a case of all hands on deck.

Howling wind and gathering darkness

When I was first shown round the boat, I remembered going down into the engine room and seeing a very large axe fixed to a side wall. This axe was now to save our lives.

Slim, the most athletic American, was roped about the waist with two of us, lashed to the boat, holding the rope ends. Slim balanced on the gunwhale of the plunging boat, wielding the axe above his head to chop through the wire and rope holding the boom to the mainsail. It was a nightmare scenario in the howling wind and gathering darkness.

Eventually Slim succeeded and the heavy boom dropped right alongside the boat into the sea with a great splash. The mainsail, now being set free, tore itself to pieces with a sound like cannon fire. No one fortunately got in the way of that thick flailing canvas.

Fate had smiled on us. The boom had not fallen back on deck but our problems weren't over.

We had to turn the boat around in the heavy seas knowing one big wave could roll us over. Luckily the motor started and we had to endure a rollercoaster ride back to Weymouth and Portland.

The interior of the boat was a complete shambles. Anything capable of coming loose had become loose. Everyone was exhausted. Joe and his crew went below. I was again on watch in the doghouse and had to make sure the helmsman stayed awake.

A casual stroller on Weymouth harbourside the following day would have been astonished to see the once magnificent boat of a day or two earlier now looking so dishevelled with rags of sails fluttering from the bolt rope, rigging littering the deck and the ugly jagged short end of the boom jutting grimly from the mast. We spent a day tidying the boat and the following day, in sunshine and on a calm sea, took FIONA back to Camper & Nicholson's mooring in The Solent for repair.

I regret losing touch with the Americans, regard the English Channel in October with great respect and think back on the lack of health and safety measures. We had no lifejackets, no lifelines, no radio, no guardrails or pulpit. I do not think the Commodore of Weymouth Sailing Club would have approved.

YAWL – in the 1950s yawls were developed for ocean racing to take advantage of the handicapping rule that did not penalize them for flying a mizzen staysail, which on long ocean races, often downwind, was a great advantage.

. . . .

LYME, ALTHOUGH A LITTLE PLACE . . .

Monmouth professed himself a great admirer of Lyme, and expressed his determination in verse of increasing its importance. All the old people repeat these lines, which are presented without comment, or the slightest intention to libel the poetical genius of that unfortunate personage:

"Lyme, although a little place, I think it wondrous pretty;
If 'tis my fate to wear the crown, I'll make of it a city."

George Roberts – "History and Antiquities of the Borough of Lyme Regis"–1834.

. . . .

MAN ON FIRE!

We next called a halt at Henstridge Ash, a tiny hamlet, the name of which may be remembered (it has no other cause for fame) owing to the long-established tradition that it was the "Virginia Tavern" there, or rather on the circular stone seat outside, where Sir Walter Raleigh was sitting quietly smoking his pipe, when the maid, coming out with a flagon of ale, alarmed by seeing a man, as she thought, on fire, promptly dashed the ale over him to extinguish it.

From "An English Holiday with Car and Camera" – 1908: by James John Hissey.

"Apologies to the purists – Henstridge Ash is in Somerset but less than a mile north of Stalbridge and well south of a straight line from Sherborne to Gillingham. Perhaps Sir Walter was unaware that he had crossed the County boundary and thought he was still in Dorset!" – Editor

THE HUNGRY HERON

He stands alone in a watery patch
hunched...watching...waiting a catch
as if, in some amazing way,
live fish would from the pebbles hatch.

One leg tucked up...the other strong...
as thin as a stick...tall and long,
it holds the shaggy figure firm...
all grey...with ash-white feathered frond.

Then quickly his body elongates...
his arched neck in a full stretched state,
a sudden dive...a massive thrust...
Poor eel! Escape became too late !

The heron swings the prize he's found,
then dashes it down against the ground...
His vigil rewarded...his skinny neck
now undulates...fulfilled and round.

Slowly he rises to take his flight...
deep beating his wings...eyes piercing and bright,
he lands in a similar shallow bed...
stealthily hunting another bite!

Kay Ennals MBE

The French have Landed

a boy's wartime memories by Bernard Palmer

What a dramatic summer I had in 1940

I was a lad of 11, living with my parents and younger sister in one of the last houses on the west side of Portland Road, Wyke Regis – just before Ferrybridge.

Shortly after the outbreak of war the authorities had billeted a young London evacuee named Terry Scanlon with us. He was eight or nine years old and soon settled in. He had a broad Cockney accent and my father used to 'pull his leg' about the spelling of his home at Chiswick, which he insisted did not include the letter 'w'. "It's Chisick Mr. Palmer. There ain't no dub yew innit." We quickly became pals and I was disappointed when his mother came and took him home after several months of the 'Phoney War'. I wonder what became of young Terry.

The full significance of the sudden collapse of the Allied Front in Belgium and France, the arrival of refugees from the Channel Islands and the evacuation from Dunkirk excited rather than dismayed our little group of youngsters – "Edgar Read's Gang" as we called ourselves.

My father, who was a fitter at the Whitehead Torpedo Works, literally just across the road, had dug a trench shelter in the back garden as the potential for really serious air raids became apparent. The concept was fine and his 'entrenching' technique had obviously been learned in 1917-18. It was roofed, as I recall, with an old door covered with several feet of earth 'spoil' from the trench and with a ladder into it at one end. Access proved difficult in the blackout whilst hurrying in our night attire and raincoats! It also had a tendency to collect water, despite a sump.

It was fairly soon filled in, having been replaced by the infinitely more comfortable compromise shelter of our big dining table, pushed into a corner, with a springmesh bedstead jammed above and a mattress shoved beneath it. My little sister, Mother and I huddled cosily inside and Dad crouched beside us when things got too noisy.

Thick bread, baths and carbolic soap for the French colonials

One morning at the time of the fall of France, when I was home from school, a convoy of vehicles pulled up in Portland Road and a number of ladies began calling at every house to inform residents that they were required to temporarily take in several

French soldiers who had just arrived from the Continent. We were allocated four and my Mother and I were astounded when they were brought to the front door.

They were French Colonial "poilus" from Equatorial Africa, still wearing their thick Bleu d'horizon greatcoats, puttees and Adrian pattern steel helmets. Virtually every house received at least a couple and we kids were fascinated by them. None could speak a word of English and I remember that several had tribal scars on their dark skinned faces.

My mother, whose grasp of French was limited to a few basic phrases picked up in France after "The Great War", was unfazed by our new arrivals and promptly assumed the role of Senior NCO !

The men were totally worn out and filthy. In unmistakable 'Pantomime' mode she led them round to the back garden and into our small greenhouse. Bringing out four kitchen chairs she bade

French Colonial infantryman
from Equatorial Africa

them sit down to await food and drink. I was set to cutting thick slices of bread whilst she filled and lit the gas fired copper which served as the universal washing machine of that era. As the water boiled Mother issued each soldier with a blanket and instructed them to undress! She warned me not to get too close as "the poor lads are lousy" and made it clear that they and their clothes would have to be properly washed before they could enter the house.

My father must have been at work at the time or he would surely have taken charge but, in his absence, the Matriarchal instinct took over.

The bemused and blanket wrapped "poilus" were fed and given coffee, Mum assuring me "the French never drink tea". Then out came our long zinc bath into which she poured buckets of hot water. Hustling me out of the way and handing them a large cake of carbolic soap and a couple of towels, she left them to their ablutions.

When the soldiers had cleaned themselves up and were sitting wrapped in towels, Mother filled the bath again and indicated the fresh water was for washing their clothes. I recall they seemed loath to do this. These essential preliminaries over, our allies were brought into the house where they promptly fell asleep.

I can't recall how long they remained with us, but eventually they were collected and departed from us with gestures of goodwill and many "Merci Madame"s.

The French were not the only military personnel billeted in our road. Sometime later, members of the newly formed Commandos were lodged for a short while with us. They came armed to the teeth. Boxes of hand grenades and Bren light machine guns were laid out along the passage and there seemed little space available for these big men and our little family.

Then off they went and we heard no more of individuals though some of their collective exploits were the subject of newspaper and even cinema reports, to boost civilian morale.

. . . .

IS THIS THE SHORTEST GHOST STORY ON RECORD?

On the short journey from Shillingstone to Blandford Forum, the man huddled in the opposite corner of the railway carriage suddenly leaned towards me and tapped me on the knee.

"Do you believe in ghosts?" he asked softly.
I shrank back, surprised. "Why I . . . Well no."
He stood up, chuckling to himself and nodding.
"Neither do I," he croaked . . . . and vanished.

From a Victorian 'Bevy of Bogeys' book- as extracted by Dave A Trench.

Bringing the World of Thomas Hardy to Life

from an interview with the playwright - by Kate Wilson

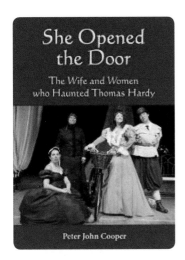

SHE Opened the Door: The Wife and Women who Haunted Thomas Hardy by playwright Peter John Cooper is proving controversial and has aroused discussion, as it attempts to understand something of the Great Man by looking at the women who surrounded him. It provides a different view of Hardy from the more conventional biographies, and the chance to read an actual working play script and understand how such a work is put together.

Peter presents a more understanding view of Emma, Hardy's first wife, imprisoned by society, circumstance and self-view within the high walls of the garden at Max Gate, the house that Thomas built for them both in Dorchester and which may have come to represent everything that was wrong with her life. The unhappy relationship between Emma and Jemima, Hardy's mother, is vividly portrayed, along with the dawning of feminism in the form of 'The Other Woman' and 'The Maid', who are both equally restrained by their situations. Hardy fans will enjoy spotting references and quotations from Hardy's own novels, poems and short stories, which Peter has cleverly interwoven into his writing.

'As a playwright, you can go further than straight biography, keeping to the facts but finding gaps where you can construct. In a play you can explore the characters and see how they might interact. I'm not a Hardy scholar but have made a reasonable guess at the truth.'

Kate Wilson for "Literature Works", which supports regional literature, caught up with Peter to chat about the research and writing process.

What drew you to write about Thomas Hardy?

I grew up in Hardy country and I've always felt that he was writing about people I knew. Some years ago I was commissioned to write adaptations of "The Mayor of

Casterbridge" and ''The Trumpet Major" and that provided me with a rather different perspective on the man and his works. I realised that Hardy was much more than the rural recorder of rural Wessex. He was an internationalist who travelled widely and met the stars of the European literary world. What's more he came to be regarded as a hard hitting contemporary artist who inspired DH Lawrence and Virginia Woolf.

Since then I've always wanted to write more about Hardy himself and when Jane McKell of AsOne Theatre asked me to write about Hardy's women I jumped at the chance. I wanted to consider how it is, that despite the central role he gives to his female characters and his support for women's suffrage he is still sometimes dismissed as a misogynist. Although Hardy himself doesn't appear, *She Opened the Door* says a great deal about his relationship with Emma his first wife, his mother and the host of women who did surround him. He is meant to be a continuing but unseen presence, rather as he seemed to be in real life.

How Important was research to the process of writing the play? How did you balance the factual with the Imagined?

I always live by the old adage that a writer should do as much research as possible and then throw it all away before starting to write. There were three strands to the research - the biographies and written records, the works themselves and the geography. The biographies I didn't use a great deal except to provide a backstop for matters of fact. The works I plundered shamelessly. I wanted to show how Hardy might have used snippets from the world around as I do. Aficionados might smile when they hear lines from the novels cropping up in the mouths of characters in my play. As to the geography, I only had to stand in the garden at Max Gate to understand how Hardy and Emma fitted into the world.

It was essential that I fit in with the facts as they are set down. So I wrote the play backwards - starting with the known facts about Thomas and Emma's life together after 1895 and then surmising how that could have come about.

There is a great advantage that a playwright has over the biographer. This is the possibility of creating a character and seeing them walk and talk in front of you. The crucial thing is that the character on stage must be credible and consistent and so, as long as he or she fits in with the recorded facts, you can find out what makes a character tick in the way that a biographer, constrained by the historical record, cannot. For me, as long as the character doesn't conflict with the record then you can explore their thoughts and impulses and parts of their character that are denied the biographer. What was extraordinary in this play was that I set off with one view of Emma but during rehearsals, actually seeing the character coming to life, I revised utterly what I thought of her. I hope I may have changed other people's views of Emma too and made her story more sympathetically received.

Can you tell us a bit about the process of writing a play; do you start with a character, a concept, or a snippet of conversation?

For me, a play grows out of a stage picture. If I can visualise a moment in the piece then the style and voice follows. I call that the taste of the play and often, if I lose my way I will go back and lick that bit again just to re-energise the process. Like any writer I keep a notebook of all sorts of scraps of conversation and events. These get jumbled up with images and scraps from the research. This jumble gets filed away in my brain where the magic chemistry happens unbidden. A stage picture and starting point comes to me when two different ideas click together and I have something new and original. With *She Opened the Door* I had the image of a furious Emma standing next to a bonfire holding Hardy's manuscript of Jude the Obscure ready to consign it to the flames. Later I saw the image that Hardy used of a sad and lonely woman on the stair at Max Gate which I amplified for Emma's soliloquy "There have always been ghosts". Between these two images, Emma came to be a living breathing woman.

You're a successful playwright; do you have any advice for aspiring writers who might wish to see their work staged?

I've always had close associations with theatre companies and I would strongly recommend writers getting involved in the grit of live theatre and learning how a play actually works on stage before sitting down in a darkened room to write. I was very lucky in that, as a young man I was able to work with some serious companies as a stage hand, stage manager and actor so I learned by watching. One of my first jobs was a stage hand on a West End show written by Alan Bennett and starring Sir John Gielguid. That was worth any amount of writing courses and theory workshops. My first writing job was, as stage manager of a regional theatre company, having to cut down somebody else's over-long script. You may not be lucky enough to get that sort of job but it doesn't stop you becoming involved with a local amateur or community company. When you've got your feet under the table you can offer to write bits and pieces. Theatre is a craft and requires a lot of technical knowledge. It's imperative you get that technical knowhow first but once you've got it you can be as creative as you like.

This book is just one of the local-interest titles published by Roving Press. For more details please visit their website at www.rovingpress.co.uk, tel: 01300 321531.

Our Annual Feast (in the Year of the Glencoe Massacre and the Salem Witch Trials)

Hayne Russell looks back...

THE earliest record of our County Dinner might well be the following advertisement which appeared in the **London Gazette** on Thursday 1st December **1692.**

"The Annual Feast for the County of Dorset will be held at Merchant Taylor's Hall in Threadneedle Street, London on the 8th instant. Tickets are to be had at Garway's Coffee House near The Exchange: at Mr. Bissom's at the Pauls Head in the Old Change: at Mr. Baxter's, Engraver, within the Middle Temple Gate and Mr. Dunford's at the Seven Stars at the corner of Katherine Street, over against Somerset House in the Strand."

There is no information to support the contention that a dinner continued to be held on a yearly basis thereafter but, if it could be proven, the County Dinner in 2014 would number 322.

. . . .

CHRISTMAS 1914

We have all read what happened between those opposing armies, and how it came unexpected, undesigned, and yet willed with all the unconscious force of their natures. Not once or twice but again and again we hear of this sudden change upon the night of Christmas Eve, how there was singing upon one side answered by the other, and how the men rose and advanced to meet each other as if they have been released from a spell.

Every one who tells of it speaks also of his own wonder as if he had seen a miracle; and some say that the darkness became strange and beautiful with lights as well as music, as if the armies had been gathered together there not for war but for the Christmas feast. . . . They sang their hymns of peace, and at the sound of them war seemed unreal, and soldiers were no longer soldiers, but men.

by journalist, critic and essayist Arthur Clutton-Brock (1868-1924)

From the Year Book – 100 Years Ago

Society historian and archivist the Rev. Dr. John C. Travell FRSA reports

Items from the Year Books for 1913-4 and 1914-5

THE Society has just elected its fifth President, Sir Stephen Collins M.P. who served as such for just two years from 1913 to 1915. Collins was born in Swanage and moved to London when he was fourteen. There he established himself as a successful business man, transporting Purbeck stone from Swanage to London. Among the many hotels, theatres and London landmarks where it was used to build were the Hotel Cecil, Hyde Park Corner, Whitehall Court, the New Gaiety Theatre, His Majesty's Theatre, the Carlton Hotel, Wyndhams Theatre, Salisbury House and London Wall Buildings. If this Society was formed to re-connect with their County men from Dorset who had moved to make their homes and fortunes in London, then through Collins, and Sir Christopher Wren whom everybody knows used Portland stone to build St. Paul's Cathedral, a remarkable amount of the land of Dorset itself has also been removed to London, where so many place names such as Dorset Square, Weymouth Avenue and Portland Place – as well as the physical fabric of the city itself – show how close the connection is between our County and our capital city.

Among the reports of Dorset Men Beyond the Seas were settlers' tales and adventures in sailing to overseas posts. Henry Facet Hurst, who was born in Blandford in 1833, had sailed to Australia in 1852. When the ship docked at Liverpool, the owners were declared insolvent, so the passengers themselves took over the ship to continue their journey, which took six months to complete. Hurst established himself as a farmer in his new land, but then a notorious bushranger named Burke invaded his home. Hurst fought to defend himself and his family, and succeeded in capturing this very dangerous criminal, but Hurst himself was seriously injured in the fight and died of his wounds.

Treves' – Three Dorset Doctors

Our first President, Sir Frederick Treves, contributed an article on "Three Dorset Doctors". This was prompted by his having met an American man in a New York Hotel. Hearing Treves' accent and realising he was English, the American asked him if he knew a place called Wynford Eagle, because, he said, that was the one place in England that he would like to visit. Treves of course, having travelled all over the County for his Highways and Byways of Dorset book, was naturally intrigued to know why this American was so interested in this small Dorset village. The man explained that he was a doctor and his hero was Thomas Sydenham who had been born there.

Sydenham, the first of Treves' three doctors, was born in Wynford Eagle in 1624 and served in the Parliamentary army during the Civil War. In July 1644 a party of 240 Royalist soldiers from Wareham attempted to loot Dorchester. The townsfolk saw them coming and sent for help from the garrison at Abbotsbury and from Weymouth. "Everybody turned out, especially the women, who armed themselves with spits, pitchforks, rolling pins and stones". The looters were pushed back to Fordington where they were met and routed by the troops from Weymouth led by the three Sydenham brothers. Thomas Sydenham went to London in 1655 and died there in 1689. He was buried in St. James' Church in Westminster. Treves says his "position among the greatest figures in the annals of Medicine depends upon very solid grounds... He is rightly known as "The Father of Modern Medicine". Sydenham rejected traditional medicine based on "humours" and based his on careful research, pioneering the methods of modern science.

The second doctor, Francis Gilson, was born in Rampisham in 1597. He graduated at Cambridge and in 1636 was appointed Regius Professor of Physics there – a post he held for forty one years, until his death in 1677. He was President of the Royal College of Physicians from 1667-1669. He wrote "a remarkable treatise" on rickets, which was very prevalent in Dorset, and also produced "a brilliant account of the anatomy of the liver". He died in London and is buried in St. Bride's, Fleet Street.

The third doctor, Nathaniel Highmore, was the son of the Rector of Purse Caundle where he was born in 1613. He graduated at Oxford and settled as a local doctor in Sherborne. He wrote about hysteria and hypochondriasis, on the cure of wounds by sympathy, on Scarborough Spa, and on the structure of the human body. "He was familiar with the anatomy of the dog and sheep...he had in fact dissected an ostrich" (thought to have come to Sherborne with a travelling fair). He became famous because he treated a lady with an abscess of the jaw by removing her left canine tooth. This resulted in him discovering a cavity in the upper jaw which became known as "Antrum of Highmore". He died in Sherborne and was buried in Purse Caundle.

The Channel Fleet – superstitions – A song of four counties

Among other articles was one by the Bishop of Durham, who had been born in Fordington in 1841. He recalled in 1860 watching, from the Ridgeway, the entry of the channel fleet into the Roads – the ships were still "wooden walls...and each moved with its pomp of white sails". An article on "Dorset Superstitions" that still survived described the belief in "ill-wishing" or "overlooking" which caused illness and bad luck. A conjuror or white witch would be consulted to remove the curse. When a horse was dying of an unknown complaint the remedy was to cut out the heart of the next animal which died and boil it in water containing sage, peppermint and onions.

"A Song of Four Counties" by Stanley Galpin and A. Kingston-Stewart had the chorus:

> Dorset gives us butter and cheese
> Devonshire gives us cream
> Zummerzet's zyder's zure to please
> The heart of a rural Dean;
> Cornwall from her inmost soul
> Brings tin for the use of man
> And the four of them breed the prettiest girls
> So damme beat that if you can!

The War and history of the Dorset Regiment

The first mention of the war is a story about a farmer and his wife being asked to take in a family of Belgian refugees. No doubt prompted by the war, the Year Book gave a full report of a lecture given to the Society in London by Colonel Sir William Watts on the history of the Dorset Regiment. The Regiment had two battalions formed from the Dorset Militia and the Dorset Rifle Volunteers. Among the many battle honours on the Regimental Colours were Primus in Indis, Plassy, Gibraltar and Egypt, Marabout, the Peninsular War, Sebastapool, Tirah, South Africa (1899-1902) and the Relief of Ladysmith. Watts comments on "Primus in Indis" that "the Territorial battalion was the first to be sent to India in the present great war, just as the old foot regiment was the first in India in 1755."

The Year Book includes a Roll of Honour; the first list of those from Dorset serving in the war. This contained some ninety names, some two or three times, including three Pearces and eight Popes – all, except one, Officers. The "Scroll of Fame" gives accounts of those already killed:

"2nd Lieut. Kenneth Aplin, eldest son of our esteemed vice-president Mr. J. Shortland Aplin; Capt. John Batten, son of our former President Col. Mountbatten; Arthur Harvey, lost at sea." An "In Memorium" lists "Capt. Wingfield Digby, 19 September 1914" and "Private W. White of Poole, whose death is given as 22 June 1914" almost two months before the war actually started on the fourth of August.

Reflecting on the first ten years of the Society, the secretary William Watkins said that the Society had endeavoured to get every Dorset Man to promote the welfare of the County; "An important function of our Society is that of benevolence. Sad homes have been comforted through the generosity of our members."

The Annual General Meeting on 11 November 1914 began with expressions of sympathy for the former President, Col. Mountbatten, whose son had been killed in action. William Watkins reported that over £200 had been raised by members for providing comforts for the men on active service. Parcels of tobacco and chocolate had been sent to the Front and an appeal had been made to wives and lady relatives of members to make mufflers, cardigan jackets, body belts, mittens (without fingers), socks etc. for Dorsets on active service. Watkins told of a letter from the Front thanking the Society for gifts. He said that every parcel had a "beautiful little label" printed with the Arms of the Society and a message "With good luck and good wishes from the Society of Dorset Men in London."

The Dorset Men Beyond the Seas reported that, on the outbreak of the war, the Penang Volunteers, commanded by Arthur Adams, a life member of our Society, was the first irregular unit to be declared an Imperial Force. Within twenty minutes of the announcement on August 5th that war had broken out 400 men had reported for duty.

· ·

DARTS AND CRIBBAGE? A BIT TAME FOR THE 18TH CENTURY

Sword and Dagger. Sherborne, Dorset, on Wednesday and Thursday, the 10th and 11th August Instant, 1768, will be played for at Sword and Dagger at the Half Moon in this town, *one Guinea* each day *for him who breaks most Heads*, and *half a Guinea for the second best Gamester*. Good encouragement will be given to the other players. To mount the Stage precisely at Three in the afternoon.

The Western Flying Post, or Sherborne and Yeovil Mercury, and General Advertizer.

· ·

DORCHESTER – 1856

Dorchester is one of the lightest, cleanest, and prettiest towns in the west of England. Its reputation for healthiness is such that Dr. Arbuthnot, who in his early days came to settle here, was driven away, saying that "a physician could neither live nor die at Dorchester."

From "A Handbook for Residents and Travellers in Wilts and Dorset".

Millers of the Establishment
The pies and demise of
a Dorset dynasty

*society member Lionel Scott Miller, grandson of the founder,
tells the family story behind Millers Pies & Sausages of Poole*

SOME of you may still remember Miller's Pies. How did it start and why did it end? A question that has gone through my mind many times.

My Grandfather, William Lewis Miller, was born in 1875 and was the illegitimate son of Elisa Miller, a native of Tyneham Village (now part of the MOD). The father was a local aristocrat where she was employed as a chamber maid. She was a good hard working mother and my Grandfather took her surname.

My Grandfather first started working at the age of 13 at Poole Potteries on the Quay as a clay puddler. He later joined a provision merchant in Poole High Street and subsequently obtained promotion to assistant manager of the shop. Eventually Mr. Harris, the proprietor, decided to retire and offered the business to him.

My Grandfather knew he was in no position to purchase the shop but when he told his wife that evening she said "The Lord will provide – I shall pray". Grandmother was very ambitious.

After church on Sunday my Grandfather usually changed his best suit for something more comfortable but on this occasion Rose, his wife, said, "Don't change this afternoon because I have arranged to meet your father to discuss some ideas I have about the offer to take over the shop".

At this time William's father was retired and living in Parkstone, within walking distance of my grandparents. On arrival at the house my grandparents were respectably entertained and Rose outlined her proposition to the old gentleman; in essence a request for an advance of £3,000 to purchase the shop, stock and considerable goodwill. Fully convinced that the plan would succeed and with a promise of repayment within 18 months the deal was done. In actual fact the loan was paid back within a year.

Grandmother always concerned herself with the local community. She was a Congregational Church supporter and was the first to be approached if there was to be a Christening, a wedding or any other festive occasion. She would be more than willing to make and supply pies for the celebration, asking only for the cost of ingredients to be covered unless for the sick and needy.

Waste not! Want not!

Sausages were already being produced in the butchery on the first floor of the shop but because of the enthusiasm for her pies Grandmother decided to make them on a more commercial basis from the scraps left over from the sausages. "Waste not – Want not" was Rose Miller's favourite saying.

At this point my Grandfather wanted his elder son, Ewart, to join him in the business. Unfortunately before this could happen Ewart was electrocuted and killed whilst working on the BBC World Transmitter in Daventry.

My father, Fred, had served an apprenticeship as an electrical engineer with the Bournemouth & Poole Electric Light Co. but, in view of the death of his brother, my grandfather insisted that he joined him in the business.

He was not treated very fairly by his father until he exposed staff theft. It seemed the quantity of goods loaded onto the delivery van did not tally with the invoices, so he arranged to meet his father on the Hamworthy side of Poole Bridge in order to stop the vehicle, which was flagged down and checked. This revealed that a number of 'unpaid for' deliveries were going to the employee's family. The staff member was dismissed on the spot and father promoted to management with a salary increase and responsibility for outside sales.

Fred used a bull-nosed Morris van for the deliveries. He had taken the doors off the van to expedite delivery into shops. I remember that as the van was returning to base it would be steaming and it was my job to refill the radiator. I would stand by with a watering can, my hand wrapped in a thick damp cloth to prevent scalding when I released the radiator cap.

The sweet smell of success – on the roof

At this time my father was experimenting with making pies on a much more commercial basis and engaged a pie maker called Mr. Cox. My father went to a trade exhibition in Birmingham and purchased a suitable oven for making pies. This was fuelled by coke and had its own chimney. Unfortunately there was nowhere to site the oven in the High Street Poole premises so father asked his friendly next door bank manager for permission to strap the oven against the bank's chimney. The manager agreed subject to the provision of slats across the roof of the bank. An electric light was installed as baking had to be done at night time and the mouth watering aroma of the cooking, drifting down into the High Street, was a talking point for local inhabitants.

The installation of the oven started the sales rolling and my father was able to buy two acres of land in Sterte Avenue with the help of his father, who complained that this was a ridiculously large piece of land. Eventually these two acres became 20 acres and in 1937 the first factory was built on the site. The ovens for this factory were huge compared with the one on the roof of the bank in Poole High Street.

Pies and sausages for the troops and black pudding for a girl

Before the Second World War broke out the business was already supplying all the Cunard Liners in Southampton with pies, sausages and other food lines. Although the business was expanding rapidly my father was protective of his local customers.

During the war the business, to a certain extent, was curtailed as meat supplies were limited to the 1937 level. However, the Miller products were great favourites with the Armed Forces and General Montgomery insisted that his troops had Millers pies when they were on manoeuvres.

Prior to the time of the D-Day landing Millers products were also being supplied to the US forces. A couple of Millers pies went into every back-pack of the invading force. It was rumoured that the smell of Millers pork pies could distract the occupants of a German tank.

During the war there was one very long air raid and all the staff took refuge in the shelter. By the time the "All-clear" sounded some of the girls were quite agitated. They rushed back to work but in the excitement one of them fell into the Black Pudding trolley and was covered in blood. This traumatised them all so much that father took pity and sent them home.

After the war Freddie Miller set about designing a larger and more modern food factory. About this time additional land was purchased to take the new factory. My father always advertised throughout the war, trying to keep the name in front of his customers with victory messages. The composition of these annoyed the family as he used to make these up whilst he was in the toilet and wrote them on Jeyes square toilet paper. Two of the slogans were, "The best that money can buy" and "As wholesome as the Dorset countryside". When the jet plane was born another slogan was "meatier than a Gloster Meteor". Once the war was over my father could buy as much meat as he required and the sausage and pie meat percentages were no longer dictated by the Government, although rationing for the public still continued until 1953.

Delivery van outside the Poole Factory

Chairman Miller's little red book

Grandmother Rose died in 1963. She was the principal shareholder at that time and under the terms of her Will various legacies were left to members of the family.

Father implored his siblings to stay with him, declaring that if they supported him he would continue running the Company and make each of them a millionaire. He was furious that they were not prepared to wait for their money.

Negotiations were started with Sir Ambrose Keevil of Fitch Lovell who bought the business a few months later.

My father continued to stay as Chairman of Millers after the takeover. Freddie, now in his mid 60s, had to pick up the reins again to train a new manager. Everything was going well and the Company was now employing about 1500 personnel. It was at this stage that my father died in a family tragedy.

At the time I was living and working in Canada where I had just returned after filming in Northern British Columbia. Naturally, I caught the first available plane to return to England and on to Poole to try and find out what had happened. My first reaction to the telegram that my sister had sent me conjured up a scene of a tragic accident because the message read "Father Dead – Mother seriously ill".

The business continued and shortly after my father's death the factory started to produce sausages on behalf of Sainsburys; something my father would never have allowed. I can still hear his voice declaring that "Nothing will ever leave this factory that is not labelled Millers."

It is with great regret that my cousins and I were not involved in the running of the business because I, for one, was a strong supporter of my father's exciting commercial ideas. To this day I still have a copy of Chairman Miller's Little Red Book that exemplifies his road map of business practice. The most appropriate saying was "Common sense is commonly rare" – which makes a suitable epitaph to his philosophy of life.

. . . .

From Ground to Air - Beam Me Up Scottie...

a prose, and poetic, portrait of contributor Lionel Scott Miller - born 14/09/1928

EDUCATED at Parkstone, Poole Grammar and Shaftesbury Schools, Lionel did his National Service with the Armoured Division of the Household Cavalry; after which he anticipated joining the family pie business; but his father was not ready to employ him.

He had a love for films so trained as a cameraman for the film industry. He was due to start work on a national film but, in spite of desperate efforts, was unsuccessful in obtaining a Union Card and was refused entry to the studio.

He had spent most of the school holidays helping a relative on a farm in Dorset so he turned to farming. He was trained in mixed farming at the Gussages near Wimborne. The farmer purchased a Leasehold Tenancy of land near Alton for his son and, always ready for a challenge, Lionel moved to Hampshire to help on the new farm. Whilst working there he met, courted and married the daughter of a local farmer.

It was after reading "Whiteoaks of Jalna" by Mazo de la Roche that Lionel decided to emigrate to Canada to continue his farming career "on the wide open plains". After a year or so as a "hired hand" Lionel still yearned to be in the film industry.

He started as an assistant cinema manager in Toronto and quickly worked his way up to Area Manager. This involved regularly working into the early hours of the morning and proved so disruptive to his family life that he decided to make a change.

Royal Canadian Air Force Badge

He joined the Royal Canadian Air Force and became an Airborne Radar Engineer working on APS 33's (the main component of airborne radar). Accepted as something of a character by his RCAF comrades they, through poetry, can continue his story, to this date, in "The Jolly Miller".

Now known as Scott, Lionel returned to his former love of films and became a freelance cameraman making films mainly for the advertising fraternity. It was whilst making one of these films that he heard of his father's untimely death and returned to Dorset.

Scott never returned to Canada and continued filming until his retirement.

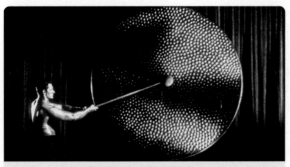

The familiar J Arthur Rank gong

The Jolly Miller

Bournemouth they tell me
is down by the sea
in far away England
where the natives drink tea!

And here in this city
where the sun shines so hot
there lived all the Millers
and Lionel Scott!

But one foggy day
(Oh! day full of sorrow)
young Lionel decided
to leave on the morrow.

"My son – oh! my son,"
was his poor mother's cry
"If you leave me tomorrow
I think I will die."

But he hardened his heart
and brushed her aside
and, true to her promise,
she laid down and died.

His father said "Lionel,
don't treat us this way.
don't wait till tomorrow
just take off today!"

The Queen sent a wire
"Stay here," she implored,
but Scott left Old England,
the place he adored.

The Canadian Army
turned out by the sea
and were ordered to welcome
this new V.I.P.

But alas all to soon
we ceased to rejoice
for no-one could figure
his clipped Limey voice.

But he didn't go back
and for this we must thank
the impeccable magnate
J. Arthur Rank.

But success still held off
till one desperate day
he thought of the airforce
"let's all kneel and pray!"

Alas, for the airforce,
he has a young wife
who seems to be pregnant
most of her life.

His nerves are all shot
his money all spent
things look really tough
for this English gent.

And yet he still chuckles
his eyes light with glee
whenever he tackles
the APS-33

His wife is still pregnant
he still has no dough
his life in a trailer
is nearly all woe.

And though he appears
a bit of a sap
I say there old fellow
He's not a bad chap.

To hell with old England
and H.M. The Queen
this Limey is staying
where the grass still grows green.

The William Barnes Society

by Richard Burleigh

THE Society's annual programme, as always, proved most enjoyable with evenings of poetry readings and music, a successful Summer Lunch, talks by Rev. Dr. John Travell (see separate Year Book article – *editor*) and Dr. Richard Bradbury, editor of the definitive six-volume edition of The Prose Works of William Barnes, and an afternoon with Tim Laycock at Max Gate. A performance by folksinger, songwriter and storyteller Graham Moore of "William Barnes and the Dorsetshire Labourer" was given at Whitcombe Church and the AGM, held at Dorset County Museum in Dorchester, was followed by a tour of the Literary Gallery conducted by Museum Director, Dr. Jon Murden.

The Annual Service of Remembrance and Thanksgiving for the life of William Barnes, conducted by Lay Minister Mr. Allen Knott, was held at the Parish Church of St. Peter at Winterborne Came, followed by a ceremonial laying of flowers in the churchyard on the graves of William Barnes and his daughter, Laura.

To complete the picture of another successful year for The William Barnes Society it should be recorded that at every event Chairman Dr. Alan Chedzoy has characteristically had constructive comments to make, and that, at the kind invitation of owner Mr. Warren Davis, several Committee meetings have been held at the beguiling Old Came Rectory – home of William Barnes for the 24 years from 1862-1886.

New members are always welcome to the Society. Subscriptions are moderate, and anyone who wishes to join should contact Mr. Brian Caddy, 31 Casterbridge Road, Dorchester, Dorset DT1 2AH (Tel: 01305 260348).

. . . .

CALLING VOLUNTEER WRITERS

from all parts of Dorset, who would like to contribute to the Year Book and carry out occasional assignments. If you can write an interesting article, conduct an in-depth interview, do simple research, would like your work to be published and have your name in print, please contact the Editor.

Benjamin Jesty : Dorset's Vaccination Pioneer

by Patrick J Pead

SELLAR and Yeatman's book *1066 And All That* contains the line "*history is not what you thought, it is what you can remember*". These words are particularly appropriate to the discovery of vaccination, Dr Edward Jenner, and a little known Dorset farmer who has been the subject of my research, writing and lecturing since 1985.

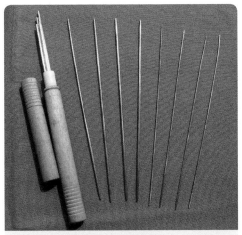

Stocking needles. The points of the narrow gauges would pierce skin easily

Benjamin Jesty lived in Yetminster, near Sherborne at the edge of the Blackmore Vale in the north of the county. Upbury, his home of medieval origin, is the oldest of a large number of houses of historical importance situated in this beautiful village and is still a working farm today. During 1774 Jesty vaccinated his wife and two sons with cowpox to protect them against smallpox in the face of an epidemic. Jesty used the point of a stocking needle to collect cowpox material from the udder of an infected cow and insert this into the arms of three members of his family.

He devised his simple and effective technique 22 years before Dr Edward Jenner who is generally regarded as the discoverer of the same procedure.

Farm workers contracted cowpox, a mild disease in humans, from contact with cattle. Milkmaids were noted for their pure complexions and the notion that cowpox protected against smallpox was part of country lore. Jesty's preventive use of cowpox was a giant leap of inspiration, and a much safer procedure than the inoculation of people with live smallpox popularised amongst the English gentry by Lady Mary Wortley Montagu in the 1720s. No *verified* use of cowpox as a vaccine is documented before Jesty. I was able to establish where his ground-breaking vaccinations took place – in a field at Chetnole, and this new information was published in the medical journal The Lancet in 2003.

Jenner rewarded – Jesty painted

After moving to Downshay Manor near Swanage in 1797, Jesty met the Reverend Andrew Bell who wrote down everything that the farmer told him about his 'experiment'.

When Jenner was rewarded with a large sum of money by parliament, Bell - together with others - petitioned with evidence of Jesty's priority but it was too late. Jenner was adjudged the discoverer of vaccination by a Commons Committee chaired by Admiral George Berkeley, the brother of Lord Berkeley who was one of Jenner's patients!

Bill Jesty with the restored canvas at a reception hosted by Wellcome in London during 2007.

Officers of The Original Vaccine Pock Institution countered this in 1805 by inviting Jesty to London where they questioned him before publicly infecting his eldest son Robert with live smallpox to prove he was immune. They considered the ingenious farmer worthy of recognition, awarding him a testimonial scroll, a pair of gold mounted

lancets and commissioning his portrait in oils by Michael W Sharp, whose sitters had included the first Duke of Wellington.

Sharp's completed canvas was exhibited at Somerset House before being hung at the Vaccine Pock Institution. When this closed in 1807 the portrait was acquired by the Director, Dr George Pearson, and when he died it was given to Jesty's son Robert. The painting was inherited by his daughter, Edith, who married a man with the surname Pope. Through this marriage, ownership of the portrait passed out of the Jesty family.

The picture was seen hanging at Chilfrome Farm, the Dorset home of Edith's eldest son Frank Ezekiel Pope, when Dr Edgar Crookshank visited Chilfrome in 1888. Records of the portrait cease at this point. It was rumoured to have been taken abroad in the distant past and was thought to be lost forever.

An international search

More than 100 years later, I began to investigate whether this portrait still existed, and if so, where it might lie hidden. Research into the genealogies of the Jesty and Pope families yielded a preliminary, but incomplete provenance. The project was given a massive boost when a list of eight people currently associated with the Pope family in South Africa was resourced. Through an extremely tenuous chain of circumstances I eventually made contact with the owner of the portrait in 2004 – his name was Charles Pope and he was living in the Eastern Cape of South Africa. He knew the story of Jesty and said that the portrait was hanging at his family home on a vast farm near Molteno about 180 miles from the coast. The picture measures 55 ins by 43.5 ins within the frame, giving an almost life-size image of the seated figure. Charles helped to complete the provenance. This is set out in detail in my recent monograph *Benjamin Jesty: Dorset's Vaccination Pioneer.* During 2006 Charles sold the portrait to the Wellcome Trust and it was returned to England. Wellcome had been "directly influenced" to acquire the painting by two of my previous publications. They arranged for a complete restoration of both canvas and frame which took almost two years.

The Jesty family, together with others, raised the funds to have the portrait exhibited at The County Museum in Dorchester in 2010. It was on show for seven months. Sharp gives us a no-nonsense character whose features have been weathered by long days of honest toil in the outdoors. Jesty's pose is dignified and exudes presence. This image reclaimed from time forms a lasting tribute to an 'ordinary' man who did something extra-ordinary. On return to London, the painting was set up in the main reading room of The Wellcome Library in Euston Road and remained there until building works began during last summer. We have also enabled the restoration of the Jesty gravestones at Worth Matravers – see illustration.

In all of this, I have been helped considerably by Bill and Vera Jesty, together with many others. My researches continue – 2016 is the bicentenary of the vaccinator's death, and I am currently working on a comprehensive biography. Benjamin Jesty is now beginning to receive more recognition. I intend to pursue that, because it is long overdue and history will be the richer for it.

For any further information please contact Patrick at pjpead@yahoo.co.uk, His monograph (ISBN 978-0-9551561-1-3) is available by order from bookshops, Amazon, or directly from Patrick.

 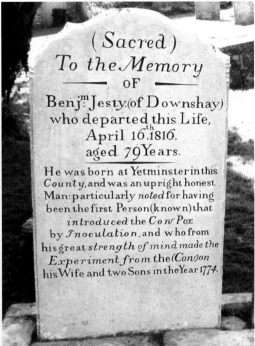

(Sacred)
To the Memory
— OF —
Benj.ᵐ Jesty (of Downshay)
who departed this Life,
April 16.ᵗʰ 1816.
aged 79 Years.

He was born at Yetminster in this
County, and was an upright honest
Man: particularly *noted* for having
been the first Person (known) that
introduced the *Cow Pox*
by *Inoculation*, and who from
his great *strength of mind* made the
Experiment from the (Cow) on
his Wife and two Sons in the Year 1774.

The inscription on the gravestone of Benjamin Jesty at the church of St Nicholas of Myra, in Worth Matravers near Swanage. Restored in 2008.

Brief biography

I was not born in Dorset, but my mother removed me from the attention of the Luftwaffe at Portsmouth in 1942 to join my expectant aunt in a rented cottage at Galton Farm near Owermoigne until the end of the war. Auntie did supply teaching at the village school where I began my education. Those times provided my earliest memories and created my love of the county which I regard as my true home, though I live in West Sussex. My career as a scientist in medicine included diagnosis and research within microbiology. The Jesty involvement began by chance – an encounter with the inscription on his gravestone – and it changed my life. My work has brought me Fellowship of The Historical Association, Membership of The Royal Historical Society, and Honorary Life Membership of The Yetminster Local History Society. I was delighted to be accepted as a "Dorset" in 2012.

Editor's Note: Forthcoming Lecture Presentations: Patrick Pead has a full programme each winter and occasionally makes the long trip to Dorset. During 2014 he is at The Puddletown Society (01305 848685) on the 12ᵗʰ March, and the Sturminster Newton Local History Society (zillabears@hotmail.co.uk) on the 13ᵗʰ March.

Home is Where the Heart is....

by David Kirkpatrick from Charlotte, North Carolina, USA

AS a boy of twelve I looked out of the porthole in the ship that brought me from New York to Southampton and, through the rain and fog, I discovered a land of Castles and Kings and it was magic.

Thirty-five years later, my wife and I spent a week in a cottage in Sydling St. Nicholas. As we turned off the A37 to wind our way into the Sydling Valley we were spellbound by the beauty and peace of the Dorset countryside. It was love at first sight. We went walking, visited neighbours and immersed ourselves in the history surrounding us. We especially loved driving the country lanes. The week went by so quickly that we hated to leave.

Two years later we returned to see if Dorset was as good as we remembered. According to my wife Jan "it was better than I ever dreamed." We went to Cerne Abbas for "Open Gardens". They were beautiful and the villagers were so welcoming that we immediately felt at home. In Long Street there was a sign that forever changed our lives - FOR SALE in the garden of the Old Police Station.

We talked of nothing else that evening....what if...how could we...should we...what would our Mothers say if we bought an English cottage?

The next day we made an offer and, after months of negotiations with thousands of details to work out, *Old Gaol Cottage* became our Dorset home.

We see ourselves not so much as owners but caretakers of this Victorian property. Our goal was to put the cottage in great shape for many to enjoy. We felt a responsibility to the village to let the cottage and encourage our guests to shop in the Cerne Store and support our pubs, tea rooms and post office. It is a great joy to know that our visitors enjoy the village experience as much as we do. Jan and I spend two months in our much loved Dorset every year but we are there every day in our minds.

Old Gaol Cottage

What enticed us to Dorset is best stated in this poem by Richard Muir.

Lodged deep in most of us is a need for roots and permanence,
And the village symbolizes a place from which strength and
reassurance may be drawn, Where the past is always present,
neighbourliness is a way of life,
and where no man needs to be a stranger.

It was Never Just Jam and Jerusalem

to celebrate its first 70 years Hilary Townsend writes about

Stalbridge Women's Institute – in war and peace

ON 7 April 1943 a good social spread of 26 Stalbridge ladies attended a meeting. It was organised by the Dorset Federation of Women's Institutes to explain the purpose, organisation and activities of the WI and how it came to be formed. It was then proposed by Miss Pearse, Headmistress of the Junior School, and seconded by Mrs. Dufosee, wife of the farmer and racehorse breeder of Stalbridge Park, "that a Women's Institute be formed in Stalbridge".

A small temporary committee got it going and by 26 April the first meeting of Stalbridge Women's Institute was held. Mrs. Dufosee was elected President and Miss Pearse and Mrs. W J Dike (great-grandmother of Andy Dike of Dike and Son Ltd.) were elected Vice Presidents. By now the WI had 50 members.

Soon it was agreed to form a Choral Society conducted by Mrs. Ethel Biddle, an accomplished pianist, assisted by Miss Amy Curtis, a local piano teacher. Shortly afterwards it was agreed to found a Drama Section with profits from its plays being given to the Red Cross. This energetic Drama Section later became a separate organisation known as The Stalbridge Players which still flourishes in Stalbridge today.

Wild Indians, wool and food rationing

Mrs. Moss, who lived at former Curate's house Laurel Bank, was an accomplished artist and every month her lovely posters appeared in Stalbridge advertising the forthcoming meeting. WI appeared prominently on them. My mother was an enthusiastic member of the WI from its inception so to tease her we said "WI – oh that stands for Wild Indians". I don't think she was amused.

The energy of the new WI was absolutely breathtaking. The first year, just before Christmas, members were issued with 11 lbs of wool to knit for the Spitfire Squadron and the Choir (plus five male voices) sang carols, raising £9 for the Merchant Navy Comforts Fund. Early in the New Year 100 members attended the first WI party with homemade refreshments, and the next day gave a party for 102 children, with homemade cakes and biscuits. Goodness knows how they managed it for food rationing had been very strict since 1939 and would remain so for years.

The streets were blacked out and, with no petrol for private motoring, Stalbridge people made their own entertainment. A committee of nine, chaired by Mrs. Simpson, wife of the manager of the National Provincial Bank, organised a Whist Drive and Dance with 28 tables of whist and a dance band of RAF personnel. This was extremely successful, making a handsome net profit of £26.6.0. Mrs. Grimes suggested at the next meeting that the WI should start a "Welcome Home Fund" for servicemen when the war ended. This was enthusiastically received and members worked tirelessly for it until peace came.

It was suggested to the WI that they should amalgamate with the Village Produce Association that cultivated Pond Close allotments and that the WI should pass its Welcome Home Fund money to the Stalbridge Parish Fund. Both suggestions were firmly resisted. Clearly Stalbridge WI had arrived. It was fiercely independent and it was going to stay that way.

WI for WCs and Men's relief relieved

In May 1944 members heard an interesting lecture on "The prospects for a satisfactory peace settlement" and the Choir sang "How lovely are the messengers who bring us the Gospel of Peace" and "The Song of Freedom". Also at this time our WI made its first determined public stand. Miss Pearse had complained that some of the Forces personnel were using the Junior School lavatories and I overheard my mother complaining to my father about the disgraceful state of the High Street first thing in the morning. Obviously men leaving the pubs the night before would simply pee in the road wherever they happened to be.

The committee prepared a letter to the Rural District Council; it was put to the next meeting, heartily endorsed and sent off. That was the public action but I am pretty sure from conversations overheard in our house that there was a private action. I believe certain determined ladies on the committee had a quiet word with the Commanding Officer of HMS Dipper, the Fleet Air Arm Station based where Henstridge Airfield is now. There were, he was told, adequate facilities in all public houses in Stalbridge and this nuisance must end. It did. Game, set and match to the WI.

There had at this time been a proposal to include women on the Rural District Council Housing Committee but it was rejected by that august body. A letter of protest was sent off at once and other WIs were informed of this action. This protest produced results. At a later meeting members gave much thought and discussion to a RDC questionnaire on housing that the Clerk, Mr. Steptoe, had sent them. Then, after peace was declared, Stalbridge Parish Council said that if the WI wished to have a woman on the Council they must support her at the forthcoming Parish Meeting. They did. They put forward two names, Mrs. Eileen Biddle and Mrs. R Meader, and both were elected.

Cinderella's Ugly Sisters – Mrs. E. Biddle and Miss W. Upton

On 6th May 1945 VE Day celebrated Victory in Europe. Victory in the Far East was still to be won but, all the same, there was tremendous rejoicing, with church bells (silent during the war and only to be rung to signify invasion) pealing out all over the Blackmore Vale. On the Saturday after VE Day the WI organised a Victory Tea for 120 children, with (of course) homemade cakes, the Parish Council gave the WI a cheque towards the expenses and sports and games continued until 6.30.

The WI meeting in July was not as well attended as usual – the meeting clashed with Polling Day. This, the ending of the wartime coalition government and the first general election since before the war, caused tremendous excitement and a sweeping Labour victory under Prime Minister Clement Attlee. Then in August the war finally ended. All but three of our servicemen returned and were presented with a worthwhile sum from the WI Welcome Home Fund to help them rebuild their lives.

Pantomime, plays, fete and festival

In August Mrs. Lovelace and her daughter Betty, who lived at what is now "Hillcrest" on Church Hill, agreed to arrange transport for a WI outing. Mrs. Newing at the Post Office agreed to post a notice and collect names of those wishing to go. Clearly the war was finally over, restrictions on private and leisure transport were being lifted and a WI outing was a ringing endorsement of peace.

The Choir and the Drama Group had helped greatly to raise money for the Welcome Home Fund and at the end of 1945 the Drama Group produced its first pantomime "Cinderella". Performances were enthusiastically received in Stalbridge, at HMS Dipper and, now that there was some petrol, at various locations round about, including travel on a lorry to perform on an improvised stage at a milk factory.

Pantomimes and plays were regularly put on by the Drama Group, while the Choir performed at the County Music Festival. A Theatre Club was formed with its first outing to the ballet in Bournemouth. A trip was organised to the Ideal Homes Exhibition in London and when the Rural District Council formed a Road Safety Committee the WI was asked to send a delegate to it.

Mrs. Hunt of Frith House offered her garden for a WI fete in 1947 on a glorious summer day. Needlework, knitting and produce stalls did an excellent trade, skittles, lemonade and ice cream were popular and teas were served on the terrace. The Matron of Templecombe Hospital judged the baby competition and the fete was opened by Mrs. Frank Byers, wife of the Liberal MP who had won North Dorset in the 1945 General Election. School children trained by Miss Upton gave a display of maypole dancing, children's sports were organised, there were ladies' and gents' ankle competitions, Mrs. Walter organised the raffles and Miss Guest presented the prizes. There was dancing on the lawn in the evening until the last bus back to Stalbridge at 10.30.

Stalbridge WI pantomime Cinderella – Fairy Queen and chorus of "Old Fairies".
Back row: Mrs. Stephenson, Mrs. Tulk, Mrs. Gawler.
Front row: Mrs. Earp, article writer Hilary Townsend, Mrs. Chandler

Stalbridge Women's Institute, begun with such enthusiasm in 1943, embraced the peace with equal vigour. Now, 70 years later, the lively WI is still there. LONG MAY IT CONTINUE.

Editor's Note: In the 2013 Dorset Year Book, Silk Hay in Stalbridge, the remarkable story of the painstaking restoration of her medieval/Tudor house by Hilary Townsend, was featured. This property is proving a popular and interesting "outing" destination for small groups of up to 23 people. No charge is made by Hilary for conducted tours although there is a pot on the table in aid of Cancer Research and her books are available for purchase.

THINKING OF DORSET

I've been thinking of my time in Dorset,
the place I love to stay.
I've been thinking of those soft round hills
that frame a twinkling bay.

I've often climbed up high to see
the strand that curls the coast,
and watch the wild waves send their spray
through coves...with pounding blast!

I've been thinking of the bracing walks,
where following a track...
I could explore some hidden beauty,
along a secret path.

I've been thinking of creation
that formed this special place,
to reflect the power of nature...
a priceless gift of Grace!

I've been thinking of the longing
that haunts me in every way...
that will not be consoled
till I return one day

to DORSET

Kay Ennals MBE

The Rifles

by Lieutenant Colonel Geoff Nicholls

THE big news for The Regiment is that it has been largely unaffected by the recent reorganisation of the Army. While many other regiments have lost battalions, The Rifles remains at its full complement of 5 Regular and 2 Territorial battalions.

Great credit must go to the "founding fathers" – the Colonels of the Regiments who decided, in 2006, that the formation of a large regiment was the best way forward. It was by no means a popular decision among the members of the Regiments at the time, with famous cap badges - including the Devon and Dorsets - being lost, but it has been proved correct. There are still changes to be made to the Territorial Army, but thankfully the only one affecting the county is that the company headquarters in Dorchester will move to Poole in due course. But we will retain a platoon presence in the County Town, unlike in Somerset and Cornwall which may well see "the axe fall" in Taunton and Truro.

Thank goodness the last year has been considerably less demanding, operationally, than previous years and that our casualty list has stopped growing at such an alarming rate. That will, of course, be no consolation to the family of Lt Andrew Chesterman from Bristol who was killed in August last year while serving with 3 RIFLES in Afghanistan, but it is otherwise a great relief. 4 RIFLES are the only one of our battalions currently in Afghanistan, where NATO forces have already handed over control to the Afghan Security Forces, so we are very much in a supporting role now. Unfortunately for them, 5 RIFLES have drawn the short straw which means they will be among the last to serve in Afghanistan, meaning a nine month tour in 2014 rather than the normal six.

The lack of operational tours does not make life any less busy, however, and battalions have spent a great deal of time training in various places around the world as well as more locally. Destinations such as Cyprus (6 RIFLES), Kenya (1 RIFLES) and Canada (5 RIFLES) sound rather appealing, but the demanding training taking place precludes much enjoyment!

Closer to home, it's been a busy year for the Regiment in Dorset. A team from 5 RIFLES visited Dorchester and gave a very illuminating presentation about their most recent tour of Afghanistan. They highlighted the particularly demanding conditions under which young men and women have had to operate in that troubled country and the audience was left with a strong sense that while some public expectations may never be fulfilled, the Army has conducted a most professional campaign.

The naming ceremony at Rifles Lane in Shaftesbury

The Lord-Lieutenant and Mayor inspecting the parade at Wimborne Minster

The Regiment has been honoured to have two thoroughfares named after it during the year – Rifles Way in Blandford Forum and Rifles Lane in Shaftesbury. There are plans afoot to have some of our battle honours marked in similar fashion in Poundbury.

The Freedom of Lyme Regis being granted by the Mayor, Cllr. Sally Holman

Freedom of Wimborne and Lyme Regis

The major event of the year was the Freedom Parade through Wimborne in late April. The Freedom had originally been granted in 2010, but at the time it had not proved possible to provide troops for a full parade. Thankfully the Mayor then, Councillor John Burden, had been re-elected for 2012-13 and was able to welcome the Regiment back. On a lovely fine spring day, members of 1 and 6 RIFLES, Dorset Army Cadet Force and the Old Comrades paraded through the town led by the combined Salamanca and Waterloo Bands who concluded a memorable day by Sounding Retreat (a music and marching display).

Another Freedom was granted in June by Lyme Regis. The Town (then a Borough) had originally been the first to grant their Freedom to the Dorset Regiment, immediately after the Second World War. This had been extended to the Devon and Dorsets in 1976 and extended further to The Rifles when they were formed in 2007. It was decided to celebrate Armed Forces Day by conducting a formal parade and ceremony to mark the Freedom. The cadets of Woodroffe School CCF (many wearing their RIFLES cap badges) formed the bulk of the parade. The Mayor, Councillor Sally Holman, presented The Rifles Deputy Colonel for the South West counties, Colonel Malachy Doran, with a splendid commemorative scroll, while she received a Silver Bugle (being the emblem of The Rifles) in return. Excellent entertainment was provided by the Salamanca Band and the Town Band.

Support for the Regiment has also been financial, particularly at charity functions throughout the year. Three years ago the charity called Care for Casualties, C4C for short, was set up. Its aim is to provide enduring support for the Regiment's bereaved, wounded and their families. Richard Drax MP has generously allowed the charity to hold an open garden on his Charborough Park estate for the past three years and these events have been run most successfully by Old Comrades from the Regimental Association branches in Gillingham and Purbeck. This year, given the late spring, there was a danger of being sued under the Trades Descriptions Act as few of the plants were in bloom, but thankfully visitors were happy to look at the carpet of bluebells and have a cup of tea.

We will remember them

Finally, it is worth taking a moment to remember some of the former members of the Dorset Regiment who have died during the past year.

Brigadier Richard Toomey receiving the proceeds of the Open Garden at Charborough Park on the roof of the Keep Museum in Dorchester

Ted Worth died in 2012, aged 92. He served throughout the Second World War, reaching the rank of WO2. Initially joining 2nd Battalion of the Dorsets, he went on to spend most of his service in 5th Battalion. In October 1945 he was awarded the Military Medal for "showing leadership and courage of an order above the average. A typical example being when his platoon suffered heavy casualties and without hesitation he rallied the remaining men and led them in a successful charge against the objective. His dash and will to victory were an example to all the men of his company." After the War, Ted served the rest of his working life in the Police Force.

Vic Farminer died in November 2012 aged 85. He served with the Royal Hampshires from 1945-48, then 1 Dorset and latterly the Devon and Dorsets, being discharged in 1968. As a Chelsea Pensioner he was very supportive of the Regimental Association and was to be seen, resplendent in his scarlet uniform, at numerous events around the county over the past few years.

John Freer-Smith died in June 2013 aged 90. He initially enlisted into the Army as a rifleman in the King's Royal Rifle Corps in 1941 and a year later was awarded an emergency commission into the Royal Sussex Regiment. Throughout the Second World War he served in Italy, Greece, Austria and Palestine. In 1946, he was granted a Regular Commission in the Dorset Regiment and served in Austria, England, Hong Kong and Minden. When the Dorset Regiment was amalgamated, John served in the Devonshire and Dorset Regiment. He was awarded the MBE for his work in recruiting. In retirement he travelled to Afghanistan three times with the charity SAFE (Support for Afghan Further Education) for whom he was the secretary. He made a significant contribution to improving the lives of the Afghan people; specifically building schools for girls and bringing fresh water irrigation systems to remote villages.

We proudly remember these gallant gentlemen and the service they gave to their county regiment.

Digging in Dorset Fifty Years Ago

by Professor Dennis Harding

THE first pre-requisite of archaeological excavation is permission of the farmer to dig on his land, which in this case was readily forthcoming, though the farmer himself seemed not fully to grasp the implications of his assent.

He was an elderly man, not obviously schooled in the prehistory of the area, and more concerned with the quality of kale which the site could produce. He knew exactly the field we had in mind, below the cross-roads at the top of Pimperne Down, as it was the one he had earmarked for this year's crop. We explained that, since the field had never previously been ploughed, even during the War, when there was an anti-aircraft post located there, the archaeological remains would be well preserved, and in any event, the surviving earthworks should not be destroyed. He fully appreciated this, and was happy that we should return later in the summer to carry out our investigations, adding, as we rose to leave, that by that time we would see for ourselves what a splendid crop of kale the field could yield. We seemed to be back to square one.

As we reached the door, his wife, a former school-teacher, and younger than him by several years, took us to one side, assuring us that all would be well, and that she 'would handle Father'. What form this 'handling' took can only be surmised, but we arrived in the summer of 1960 to find the site untouched, though surrounded by kale as far as the eye could see.

Our relations with the farmer remained cordial throughout the three season's excavation, though the equilibrium was threatened the following year from an unexpected source. On arriving at the farm, Jimmer, as he was known locally, was in a state of high dudgeon, waving forms in triplicate at us, and blaming us for some as yet unexplained intrusion upon his civil liberties. 'They can't do this', he protested, 'it's my land'. What could who not do, we enquired? 'Put pylons across my best kale field!' he raged. 'It's my land!' Indeed, I assured him, they could not. Not because it was his land, though I could see the justice of his case, but because it was now a Scheduled Ancient Monument. He hesitated for a moment, before seeking our assurance once again that the notice he had received from the Electricity Board was none of our doing. On the contrary, I confirmed, we would notify the appropriate authorities, and ensure the application was denied. From that moment a bond was forged which served us well to the end of the excavation.

Many years later, I re-visited the site, by which time the farm had doubtless passed to another generation. There were still no pylons. But nor were there any surviving earthworks. Just an uninterrupted vista of the finest kale you could ever wish to see.

"Weren't nothing before the Romans!"

I have frequently found that, notwithstanding our sense of national history that may be the envy of transatlantic tourists, many people find the perspective of time beyond a few generations hard to grasp. Thus it was with Jimmer, but more so, as we discovered when we showed him some of the finds from our first season's work. I offered my considered opinion that they dated to the early Iron Age, in round figures, five hundred years before the Romans. 'Before the Romans!' he retorted with incredulity. 'Get away wiv yer! Weren't nothing before the Romans!' Indeed there were, I assured him, but he remained unconvinced as I attempted to summarise the current conspectus of pre-Roman Britain. Finally, he became reflective, and I sensed I had made a breakthrough. 'If what you say is right,' he said slowly, 'then I don't reckon as how there'd be many folk around as would remember that.' He was not trying to be funny. For Jimmer there was his dad, his dad's dad, and possibly his dad's dad's dad. And then there was King Alfred and the cakes, and before that the Romans.

This chronological compression of history was known to the actor and raconteur Bernard Miles, who about that time recorded tales in the persona of Nat Titlark of Ivinghoe in Hertfordshire, a village that 'was built by the Vikings in the 'leventh century, afore the railway come'. We packed the finds back into their boxes and made our polite exit. For the moment I felt that my crusade to enlighten the world to the fascination of archaeology had received not just a mild setback, but a resounding kick in the pants.

Shop, post office, pub and feral feline pets

The bridge was the focal point in the village of Pimperne at that time. It was not a particularly auspicious bridge; in fact, it was a broken down wooden one, designed only for pedestrian traffic across a stream between the Post Office and General Stores on one side and the Farquharson Arms on the other. By night the bridge was lit by the pale green glow of the flourescent tubes which outlined the village pub like varicose veins. In days when archaeological excavations depended upon volunteer labour, and cheap local accommodation, it was customary to make early acquaintance with the publican and the vicar, in the hope that a notice posted in their respective establishments would attract the names of local families willing to offer bed and board at a modest rate. For reasons which I cannot now recall, but to our eternal relief, we decided first to try the pub. The lounge bar was crowded with officers from the local army camp, but the public bar seemed well patronised by locals, and it was here that the landlord readily agreed we could post our notice. He proved a stalwart supporter of the excavation, providing

Sign for the Farquharson Arms - Trish Steel
CC-BY-SA-2.0 , via Wikimedia Commons

introductions to various individuals who helped our cause. But an approach to the vicar he did not advise. Leaning across the bar, with a cautious glance to see who might be listening, he confided, 'He's shot his bolt in this village!' No further intelligence regarding the nature of the bolt-shooting was forthcoming, but it sounded like advice worth heeding.

Some weeks later, while work was in progress, an elderly SS Jaguar drove on to the site, and a figure emerged with outstretched hand. 'How do you do? My name's Folland-Wrigley (not his real name, I hasten to add, though similar). I'm the local incumbent. Not a wealthy parish, you understand, but then I have my private means.' As an opening gambit, calculated to engage parishioners, I could see this was hardly a bulls-eye, and we could well appreciate how such an approach in a rural community might add up to a 'shot bolt'.

At first sight, the village stores was not an obvious candidate as commercial entrepreneur of the year. The window display, which was thick with dust, consisted of a pyramid of Izal toilet rolls with a backcloth of crepe paper, crowned on the top shelf by a galvanised iron bucket. The store was run by an elderly and amiable couple. His baldness on top was compensated by an abundant walrus moustache, while she had her hair tied neatly in a bun, so together they brought to mind the figures that used to move in and out of old-fashioned barometers depending on whether it was going to rain or shine. The shop was fairly cramped, not least behind the counter, a difficulty which frequently led to confusion as he leaned backwards over the counter to compensate for his short-sightedness while the frustrated customer pointed vainly at some commodity on an upper shelf. Meanwhile, she would endeavour to direct the old gentleman's gaze, but, being dentally disadvantaged and given to agitation, her advice was less than coherent, especially if she was standing on the side in which he was hard of hearing.

The store had originally been a bakery, and at the back it was a maze of passages, stacked high with cardboard boxes and vegetable produce. In the parlour, a short-cased clock hung in the corner, next to a vintage telephone of the kind in which the receiver was detached from the upright stem and held horizontally to the ear. The table was littered with orders and bills, all kept in place by brass paperweights. With the advent of inspectors, the bakery had closed, to the dismay of all their customers, for whom the occasional cockcroach was a small price to pay for fresh-baked bread. The outbuildings had thus been adapted for hens, which consistently laid eggs too large for the Egg Marketing Board to accept. No-one knew quite why this was so, though it was rumoured that the old man's nightly trip across the bridge for bottles of stout was not exclusively for his own consumption, but the result was that he did a brisk trade in fresh 'varm' eggs that were infinitely preferable to the several weeks old version of fresh eggs distributed by the Board.

Farquharson Arms, Pimperne - Trish Steel CC-BY-SA-2.0 , via Wikimedia Commons

Amid the general chaos, the only member of the household that seemed to have it made was the cat, who, having been made redundant by the closure of the bakery, now spent a leisuredly retirement in the window, sunning itself on the top shelf by the galvanised bucket. I only once saw its composure ruffled, when it stretched and rolled over in the sunshine. With a look of utter disbelief on its face it disappeared from sight in a cascade of toilet rolls, followed by the clatter of the bucket, as the prized display collapsed. We all watched in stunned silence until a movement behind the debris was followed by the appearance of a paw, and then a furry face with a bemused expression that comic cartoonists would have depicted with stars and other symbols, as the unfortunate moggy hauled itself back on to its perch.

Prior to its arrival in the village stores, the cat had evidently led a full and eventful life, one of three that lived in the local pig-farm, where they were fed regularly by one of the labourers. The man, however, was dismissed, and after several days without food, the cats decided to decamp, and seek alternative accommodation in the village. The three arrived at the wooden bridge, where they stopped to consider their options. One chose the warmth of the bakery, and ultimately the comfort of the window shelf; a second turned in the opposite direction, and found a home in the village pub, while the third remained in the road, undecided, and was run over by a lorry. Though this cautionary tale has the hallmark of anecdote, its authenticity was nonetheless affirmed by several of the villagers, and, of course, by the two survivors themselves.

Where there's muck there's money

We had hardly been on the site for more than a day or two when we encountered Mole. That of course was not his real name, though by way of introduction he had produced his business card, which styled him as a 'manure and clinker merchant'. He acquired the name because of his resemblance to an animal character from childhood fiction, his pear-shaped figure clad in blue overalls held high up his chest and back with straps over the shoulders. The ensemble was completed by heavy ex-army boots and a cloth cap. His language was admittedly more colourful than would have been suitable for a children's story, and instead of smoking a briar pipe, he rolled his own cigarettes, spitting adroitly on the paper to stick them down in a manner which would have been out of keeping in the polite society of animal fiction.

His interest in the site was the rich downland turf- 'mould' as he called it- which he sold to tomato growers in the local market towns. The tools of his trade were essentially two, his spade, worn down through years of use to a short, crescentic blade, and his 'prung', with which with minimal effort he flung the sods into his 'lurry'. He seemed to spend hours leaning on his spade, holding forth about the political situation or life in general, to the considerable distraction of our own work effort, yet his rhythm of work was such that he easily loaded his five ton truck to well above cab height by the end of the day. In his youth, he claimed, he could load it and return to his depot three times a day, but the years were beginning to take their toll.

Amiable though he was towards us as fellow diggers of soil, he did not hold humanity universally in high regard. He was notably uncharitable towards the farmer's wife, whom I suspect was sufficiently astute to fathom his somewhat dubious business practices. With a characteristic local ability to invert the nominative and accusative, he pronounced emphatically, 'her's a tartar, her is; you don't want to get across she'. His other principal aversion was the officer corps, which included a retired RAF Group-Captain who was one of our volunteers, whom Mole persistently referred to as 'th'old admiral'. This antipathy evidently stemmed from his wartime experiences in North Africa, where it seems he also drove a lorry. He recalled an occasion when he was instructed to dispose of a load of unexploded bombs. 'This officer picks me, because, says he, there's no point in all of you getting killed. Well, I ask you, talking to me like that...', protested Mole, with the deep, throaty growl with which he habitually prefaced and ended his observations on life.

Mould was evidently not his only line of business. He claimed to have acquired forty fine pine trees from the garden of an elderly lady in Bournemouth by convincing her that they had the 'pine tree disease' on the basis of some perfectly natural discolouration near their roots. He also regularly acquired bales of straw, and was once reckoned to have bought a load of straw for £5 during a particularly good summer, and sold it back to the same farmer for £15 the following winter. One morning I arrived at work early, to find Mole's lorry standing empty by the gate. Spotting a movement beneath a tarpaulin which was covering the baling machine, I waited for him to emerge. Momentarily embarrassed by being caught in the act, he confided that the farmer had agreed to sell him some bales. 'Well,' he explained with his usual growl, 'you see, they balers got like a speedometer on 'em, what tells you the number of bales...' I began to get the drift of the transaction, and enquired no further. But after that, Mole very obligingly agreed to cut his mould in neat, ten-foot squares in areas where we planned to excavate.

As time passed, Mole began to take an interest in the excavation. He never really believed that there was no money to be made from archaeology, and clearly thought that I was just being canny in not confiding in him. He carefully collected any pottery sherds he found while stripping turf, and whenever he struck stone he would advise us that 'they Romans been under here; I keep hitting 'em with me prung.' Whenever visitors arrived on site, he enjoyed posing as an authority, though he spun the most outrageous tales to anyone gullible enough to listen. I recall overhearing him on one occasion explaining to an admiring group how we had dug up the skeleton of an old gypsy-woman. 'How did you know it was a gypsy-woman?' asked one. 'Ah, well,' growled Mole, 'she must have been, see, because she had a clothes-peg clipped to her nose.'

One winter, Mole was stricken by illness, and when he arrived for our final season, he was a pale shadow of his former self. 'It's me lungs,' he explained in a hoarse whisper. He continued to come for his mould, but unlike former times, he really did spend long periods leaning on his prung. One afternoon, just before the excavation ended, I found him sitting on the running-board of his lorry. 'It's no good,' he announced, coughing, 'I got to give up.' Then, remembering that I too earned my living by digging, he looked up and asked, 'You don't want to buy a good business, I s'pose?' adding a price for the lorry and 'goodwill'. I declined his offer, not reckoning the 'goodwill' of his business to be its strongest suit, though I have sometimes reflected how profitably I might have combined the mould business with archaeological fieldwork.

General Mayhem and Major Confusion with the Army

For two summers the entire excavation team was billeted in the Officers' Mess of 30th Royal Signals, which was one of the regiments based at the local army camp. My co-director on the excavation had served with Signals during his National Service, and still held a reserve commission, as a result of which he had been able to negotiate generous facilities at a very moderate rate through the goodwill of the Officer Commanding. We even enjoyed the services of a cheerful Irish batman, who brought sweet tea first thing in the morning, announcing that it was a lovely day, whatever the weather was like outside. Certain conventions had to be observed, of course, particularly in respect of the female members of our team, who, unlike Major Gatling's alsatian, were not permitted to use the officers' anteroom. In most other respects, however, attitudes towards our civilian intrusion were fairly relaxed. If we needed transport, it was probable that the ration truck would coincidentally be needed for an exercise in our locality; when our polythene rain-shelters threatened to blow away in the wind, camouflage netting proved an ideal means of securing them.

When we were particularly short of labour, a troop of 'volunteers' appeared on the site in the charge of a corporal to lend a hand. They were not the most committed workforce I have ever used, though what they lacked in subtlety they made up for in raw enthusiasm. 'Don't you 'ave a machine to dig 'oles for you, sir?' asked the squad humourist, wielding his pick and shovel like a soul in torment. I replied that a machine might damage sensitive archaeological deposits, and that in normal circumstances digging by hand was therefore preferable. Undeterred by the hint, he continued his patter. 'The army's got a machine for digging 'oles, hasn't it, Corp? They calls it a soldier.' 'Shut up, Signalman Herbert!' barked the corporal, as I retreated from the field of battle.

Perhaps the most useful piece of equipment provided by the army was a telescopic tower, mounted on a three-ton truck, which we used for high-angle photography. The platform, which was not much more than four feet across, with a low guard rail, was supported by three hydraulic legs, and at sixty-five feet swung appreciably in the breeze in spite of the struts which held the truck secure. We had noticed it parked near the parade ground, and enquiries revealed that it had originally been used by the German army in wooded terrain for spotting aircraft. It proved ideal for our purposes, which were to record from high angle the post-holes in the chalk of a large, circular Iron Age house. Nearly fifty feet in diameter it was one of the best preserved plans of such a building ever recorded, before or since. In nearly forty years of excavation I was never able to match the photographs which my co-director took from this precarious vantage-point.

I subsequently learned that the truck had later been involved in an incident of the kind that must be hard to explain to an insurance company. When the tower was lowered, it hinged forward to rest on the driver's cab. Apparently, the truck was stopped in a line of traffic in Andover when the driver's mate inadvertently triggered the mechanism that operated the tower. Before the crew could grasp what had happened and take remedial action, the tower had extended forward until the inevitable point of imbalance was reached, whereupon the platform came to rest on the roof of a car several ahead in the queue, the intervening vehicles escaping unscathed. I do not know what became of the truck, or the driver, but we were not able to secure its use again.

It is a well-known adage that an army marches on its stomach, but reflecting upon the size of the packed lunches which were daily delivered by the ration truck to the site, I often thought it was remarkable that the army could march at all. Apart from regulation sandwiches, the large brown-paper bags also contained pies, hard-boiled eggs, sausages, fruit and sweets, and on one occasion something that looked suspiciously like small steamed puddings. Since we never managed to eat it all anyway, and the little puddings did seem out of place without a jug of custard, I asked the corporal whether he was quite sure they were intended for us. Indeed he was, and so I thought no more about it. As we relaxed in the downland sunshine at lunchtime, and the village dog munched his way ruefully through umpteen puddings that members of the team had discarded, a cloud of dust advancing rapidly up the road signalled the arrival of a very distressed corporal. 'Them little pudding things, sir,' he spluttered, 'they're meant for the officers' lunch!' What could be salvaged, was, but it would have taken liberal quantities of custard to conceal that there had been a culinary calamity of the first order.

During the summer leave period there was not much activity in the camp, and for a few days the Medical Officer spent some time working with us on the excavation. The presence of an army ambulance on site might have led to rumours spreading through the village, but it was reasonably well concealed by a tall clover crop within which we had been allowed by the farmer to open one of our trenches. One afternoon, a jeep appeared through the gate, driving heedlessly through the clover towards us. I waved the driver down, and, explaining that the farmer regarded clover as a crop, not a weed, asked his business. The MO was needed urgently at the camp, he reported. We knew that Signalman Herbert had been absent without leave, and had heard how he had turned up on the parade ground in a disorderly state minutes before an important inspection. We also knew that, when the RSM had spotted this nasty intrusive sight, and had bellowed at him to b****r off, Signalman Herbert had done just that, for several more days. Finally, it seemed the prodigal had returned, to be marched to the guardroom to explain his conduct to Major Gatling. It was at this point that the man's self-discipline had snapped, and he had flung the table at Major Gatling. It was the consequence of this incident that required the MO's attention, though it was not immediately apparent for whom the MO's services were most urgently required. The outcome, of course, was not our concern. But I have no reason to believe that the Major did not enjoy a happy retirement.

St Peter's Church, Pimperne - Trish Steel CC-BY-SA-2.0 , via Wikimedia Commons

Bobbies and Borstal Boys

Relations between the camp and the local market town were generally cordial. On Saturday nights, of course, it was not uncommon for a disorderly soldier to end up in the cells, and the Station Sergeant was well-known to most of the officers. So when the excavation yielded part of a human skull, they were adamant that we should report the matter to the Sergeant personally. Strictly, it was true that human remains should be reported to the police, but when their archaeological context is beyond doubt, reporting such finds might be thought to be a wilfully vexacious waste of police time, which was exactly what the officers intended it should be. The Sergeant was suitably impressed by the news that human remains had been found on the Downs, and selected a fresh pencil to enter the report in his register. First, he would require our names, addresses and occupations. Once he had mastered the spelling of 'archaeologist', he proceeded (policemen in those days always 'proceeded' to do things) to ask us if we could ascertain the cause of death. Certainly, I replied. 'He was pole-axed. Skull split vertically in half.' 'Foul play' was duly entered in the log. And could I perhaps hazard a guess as to when this had happened? I could not be precise, I explained, but I would reckon between 2000 and 2500 years ago. He turned crimson. 'You've made me write in the book!' he bellowed. 'What am I going to tell the Inspector?'

In general, the local constabulary was not unduly taxed in upholding law and order in rural Dorset, so the arrival of several squad cars and a force of policemen on site excited no small interest in the locality. Ironically, it had nothing to do with the excavation, other than by the quirk of coincidence. In search of additional manpower, we had recruited from a Borstal near Shaftesbury a daily detail of diggers, who were allowed to work on the site under strict supervision. They were a somewhat inconsistent workforce, since the privilege of outdoor activities was withdrawn if individuals misbehaved back at the camp, or they might opt out if more interesting activities like football were available.

Unfortunately, it transpired that a pair of new inmates determined to break out within hours of their arrival at the Borstal, and quite by chance chose to head southwards on a course which brought them directly past the excavation. Had they not been city lads, they might have realised that the neighbouring pig farm, which boasted the largest herd of breeding sows in Europe at the time, afforded them ideal refuge from the pursuing tracker dogs. Instead, they chose the road, and were caught in a barn a few hundred yards away. Though the incident had no direct bearing upon our labour-force, the experiment of archaeological therapy for youthful malefactors was abruptly abandoned.

In retrospect it is surprising that such an irregular work-force so inadequately funded should have achieved as much as it did, and in some respects archaeological fieldwork in the early 60s had more in common with the era of General Pitt-Rivers' excavations on Cranborne Chase than it has with modern, development-led archaeology. Shortly after the conclusion of the excavation, at a meeting of the premier national archaeological society in London at which I had presented the results, one senior Fellow expressed regret that the younger generation was apparently unwilling to invest its private income in field research, a remark which seemed to me to rank for crass insensitivity along with Mr Mervyn Griffith-Jones' celebrated question to the jury at the Lady Chatterley trial of the same period, whether this was a book they would wish their families and servants to read? Not everything has changed for the better, but some things certainly have.

Dorsetman, Professor Dennis Harding was an undergraduate at Oxford when the excavation at Pimperne took place (1960-1963), after which he moved first to Durham University and then to Edinburgh where he held the Abercromby Chair of Prehistoric Archaeology for thirty years from 1977 to 2007.

Although it was not the first field project he had organised, he says "it is probably the one that I look back on with the greatest pleasure".

NB: The landlord of The Farquharson Arms in Pimperne at the time was our own Hon. Life Member, Past Chairman and Society Stalwart, Roy Adam MBE.

The Great War Comes to Dorchester

by Brian Bates BA, DMA

WITH the one hundredth anniversary of Britain's declaration of war on Germany closing fast, it is an opportune time to look back and see how our county town reacted.

If the pages of the *County Chronicle*, published less than a week before the outbreak of war, are anything to go by the people of Dorchester had little indication of what was around the corner. The County Hospital held its annual harvest festival and Mr Hawkins, gardener to Denzil Hughes-Onslow, the owner of Colliton House, took first prize in the local sweet pea grower's competition, unaware that within a year his employer would lay dead in France, with a bullet in his head.

In the Chronicle's advertising columns Mr Fred Dabinett, decorator and paper hanger, announced that he was now starting up his own business in the town and doubtlessly hoped that his two sons, Bert and Reg, would join him. Of the two brothers, only Bert returned home from India with the 4th Dorsets, leaving behind the body of his Reg, who died after being bitten by a rabid dog, in Mesopotamia.

It was also that time of the year when the grammar school held its prize giving. On Monday the 27 July the headmaster stood up and gave his annual speech. He praised, in particular, two members of staff for their work with the Officers' Training Corps and reiterated his view that the OTC had a high educational value in its influence on the general character, demeanour and methodological habits of the boys. He was particularly pleased that it had received a good report following a recent inspection by the War Office. In July 1917 the headmaster once again gave his annual address but this time it had had a different tone. In addition to the usual plaudits to scholars and staff it contained the roll of honour of 20 former pupils who had died as a consequence of the War.

Dorchester – home to the Dorset Regiment

Of course, Durnovarians were used to seeing men in uniform around the town. The Depot Barracks, home of the county regiment, and the adjacent Royal Artillery Barracks were located on the western edge of Dorchester, just a few hundred yards from the town centre. Consequently, there were always soldiers to be seen in the streets. They attended services at Holy Trinity, the garrison church, and frequented local pubs; the Old Ship Inn in High West St was a favourite.

Many a soldier fell for the charms of a local girl and married her, some with more haste than others. The sound of the army was ever present, be it when the bugle sounded reveille each morning or the clip clop of horses' hooves as an artillery battery moved through the town. The sound of a military band was often heard in the Borough Gardens on a Sunday afternoon, or at a 'smoking concert' in the Corn Exchange.

On 6 July, 1914 the men of the 3rd Dorsets had assembled at the Depot Barracks before going to their annual training camp on Salisbury Plain, the Dorchester Company commanded by Capt. H Duke and Lt G Symonds, both prominent men in the town. Because the conflict broke out whilst they were training, they were sent directly oversees, some not seeing their families until the end of the War and others not at all.

When War did arrive, the usual military presence in the town took on a new dimension. When the next issue of the Chronicle was published, on 6 August, two days after Britain entered the conflict, the Dorchester pages were dominated by military matters, signalling the whirlwind that was to affect radically all aspects of life. Six months later the Chronicle was able to comment that, 'The War has changed our habits along with our mood. Instead of a round on the golf links, a spin with the motor cycling club, a trip to Bournemouth or Weymouth, afternoons are now devoted to sterner stuff, defence of the Motherland.' [1]

Hundreds of new recruits, as well as existing regular soldiers, could be seen making their way to and from the Depot Barracks, and 'Debonair and active recruiting sergeants, flaunting their alluring ribbons,' [2] were abroad in the town, stopping any likely candidates for military service. Existing Territorial Army brothers William and Reg Membury turned up at the Depot Barracks together to enlist with the Dorsets. Reg was refused because he had a heart murmur but his brother went with the 1st Btn to France, where he was killed on the first day of the Battle of the Somme. The Chronicle described Dorchester as being like 'a leagured town in the bustle, excitement, and the many and varied uniforms seen in the throng, hurrying to and fro.'[3] Members of the Reserve of Officers hurried to the Depot to learn of their new duties and Reservists were reporting to the Barracks to be clothed and armed. One batch of five officers and 100 men left by train from Dorchester West Station, on their way to Belfast to join the 1st Dorsets, while others had shorter journeys, to training camps in the county or other parts of the country.

Prisoners of war arrive

One arrival of men caused considerable excitement in the town when, on 10 August, 1914, a group of 18 Germans stepped down from a train at Dorchester West railway station as prisoners of war. The Chronicle reported that they were viewed by hundreds, with a mixture of curiosity, amusement and foreboding. This was the first contingent of thousands of foreign prisoners who were to find a temporary home on the

Dorchester recruits to Kitchener's New Army being escorted to the Depot Barracks by pipers of the Scottish Fusiliers - August 1914. (from the private collection of Mrs. S. Poulter).

site of the artillery barracks, throughout the war. At its height, the prison camp housed almost four and a half thousand men. Durnovarians treated the next consignment of 'outsiders' somewhat differently. These were wounded prisoners of war, to be treated in one of the town's military hospitals. Colliton House was the main hospital and there was another in Durngate St, opposite Wollaston House, superintended by Mrs Acland.

Dorchester's women soon mobilized themselves. Some knitted socks for soldiers, some collected eggs for the National Egg Collection, whilst others, like Mrs Wynyard, organised events to raise money for the Dorset Regiment Comforts Fund. And it was not long before women were taking the place of men in the workplace. Channons coachworks employed an all female workforce, making parts for gun carriages, as did the Lott and Warne Foundry. They also served in local shops, a job done predominantly by men before the War.

It was also was a time of sacrifice. Horses of all types and from all sources were commandeered. There were even stories of animals being taken from their shafts in the streets. 'Gentlemen' were encouraged to hand in their field glasses to the military. Local sporting events were suspended and day trips to Weymouth and Bournemouth were cancelled, as the trains were needed for carrying troops. Mr Allen the mayor, told the townsfolk that, 'There is not the slightest reason for panic. Full arrangements are being made to meet the situation. Do not store goods or create an artificial scarcity to the hurt of others. Remember that it is an act of mean and greedy selfish cowards.' [4]

The County Regiment was scattered around the globe, fighting in France, Belgium, Turkey, Mesopotamia, Egypt, Palestine and even Russia, and was not long before the casualty lists began to appear in the Chronicle, and telegram boys were visiting houses with the dreaded telegram. No stratum of Dorchester society was exempt. Alfred Pope, the brewer, lost three sons, whilst Thomas Benjafield, who ran his bakery from what is now the Baker's Arms, lost two.

As the death toll mounted, the Chronicle and this Society's Year Books recorded the fallen. The 1917/18 Year Book recorded the deaths of two brothers of Arthur Martin, one of the Society's 'most enthusiastic members,' who lived in America where he raised considerable funds.

Unveiling of Dorchester's town memorial on 24 May 1921. (source Mrs. P. Collins).

A mother's elegy for her sons

Two hundred and eighty-four men and one woman appear on our county town's Great War memorials and as our awareness of that terrible conflict comes into greater focus this year, the effects it had on Dorchester people cannot be better encapsulated than in the epitaph which Lavinia Hare placed in the Chronicle, in memory of her two sons:

Could their mother have clasped their hands,
The sons she knew so well.
Or kissed their brow when death was near
And whispered 'my sons farewell'.
I seem to see their dear sweet faces
Through a mist of anxious tears.
But a mother's part is a lonely heart
And a burden of lonely years.
We miss you, for we loved you,
As memories we recall.
The parting with our dear ones
Was the saddest day of all.

This article is based on the writer's book,' Dorchester Remembers the Great War.' It is available from the author, (Tel: 01305 263824) priced £12.99, including p&p. (UK only). It is also available from bookshops and from Amazon. [1] Chronicle 4/3/1915. [2] Chronicle 15/7/1915. [3] Ibid. [4] Chronicle 13/8/1914

Editors Note: Brian Bates gives fully illustrated talks on Dorchester's rich history. Each hourly talk can usually be modified for each group and is subject to a charitable donation and minimal travelling expenses.

Talk 1 - An Imaginary Walk through 17th Century Dorchester

In the early 17th century Dorchester was seen by many as a hotbed of puritan revolution. Through an imaginary walk through the town we will see how Durnovarians were affected by, and contributed to, the cataclysmic national events that would eventually lead to the English Civil War. We will also see how the high and the low born dealt with the every day tribulations of hunger, sickness and crime.

Talk 2 - Dorchester Remembers the Great War

As a garrison town, the outbreak of WW1 had more significance the inhabitants of Dorchester than most other towns. At the end of conflict 285 names were added to the town's various war memorials. Through the stories of some of those who perished in that terrible conflict this talk shows how their families and the local community dealt with the tragic losses.

Talk 3 - When the Germans Invaded Dorchester

The invasion began in August, 1914, when 18 German prisoners arrived in Dorchester. By March, 1919 4,500 foreign nationals were incarcerated in one of Britain's largest POW camps, situated on the outskirts of the town. We will see what life was like in the camp and how Durnovarians dealt with the extraordinary situation they found themselves in.

Talk 4 – Thomas Hardy's Dorchester

Thomas Hardy's life spanned the 19th and the 20th centuries. This talk shows what Hardy's Dorchester was like at this time and how the town dealt with the changes that were taking place in society.

Talk 5 – Lives around the Borough Gardens

Dorchester's Borough Gardens is a fine example of Victorian pride. This talk illustrates a history of the gardens and then takes a peek through the curtains of some of the splendid villas surrounding the gardens, to view the people who lived in them.

Brian can be contacted by telephone on 01305 263824, or e,mail at brianbates@trayfoot.co.uk to discuss requirements and terms.

THE CHURCHYARD, SYMONDSBURY

Through the side gate,
and suddenly in the deep cool
of the yew path,
the air is a mesh of insects.
The soft bulk of bumble bees,
two butterflies chasing upwards,
a skittish double helix,
rising white winged into the blue.
And on the breeze
The steady drone of flies, quartering among trees.

Along the yew path
the trees are wire bound,
branches held close to trunks,
strays lopped at chest height,
keeping leaves from faces passing through.
Straight as soldiers on parade,
straight as poplars, a green guard of honour,
but for one cut to the ground,
short brown stump obvious as a missing tooth.

Reaching the church door
and suddenly locked in a slab of sunshine,
the air is hot and still.
Somewhere a dog barks.
Beyond the solid front gates
wrought in heavy iron by a Sprake,
his family buried just a perch* away,
beyond the rounded steps beyond the road,
a metal ladder clatters at the school wall.

Bright white overalls
glare in sunlight, a furnace of effort,
as white gloss goes onto window frames
and down pipes, electric white,
almost painfully bright
against the warm sandstone of ancient classrooms.
Another day or two will see it done,
and then the avalanche of children.

The sun beats in a pale blue sky.
Thin ring of aluminium on stone,
doves soft calling,
the sudden clatter of wings among the trees.
Summer winding down
and the world holds its breath.

by Paul Snow

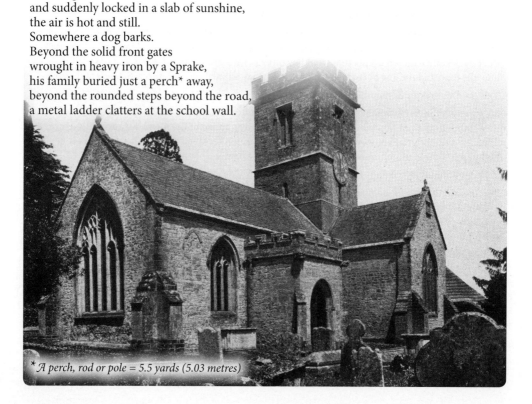

*A perch, rod or pole = 5.5 yards (5.03 metres)

My Father – the 1st Tank Attack - Lawrence of Arabia - and Me

as told to the Editor by Society Member Don Reiffer

IT was a black day for the British Army when the Somme offensive opened on 1 July 1916. With little ground gained, nearly 60,000 men had fallen; a third of them killed.

By September, Sir Douglas Haig, Commander-in-Chief, had commanded a wide front that had advanced less than four miles at unimaginable cost in lives, mutilation and suffering. Demolished farms and ruined villages, wrecked supply wagons, horse carcasses, abandoned equipment and the unburied dead lay everywhere across a devastated landscape.

He decided to push ahead anyway in an attempt to destroy the German Army and an assault was planned as part of a simultaneous offensive with the French.

Against expert advice he was determined to use the new British super-weapon – TANKS. Only a few were available and the crews were not fully trained.

One of their number was **Alfred Henry "Roy" Reiffer,** son of a London sponge and chamois importer from the Old Kent Road.

It must have been hellish inside a tank. The incessant noise from the exposed engine, the grinding and screaming gears, the foul air polluted with fuel, exhaust fumes and cordite smoke, and limited vision through narrow openings in the armour plating. For Roy the constant lurching, sudden stops and erratic movements of the iron leviathan must have been uncomfortably dangerous having his back only inches from the hot engine. He was a starboard gunner and this was before the attack.

About 6.30am on 15 September 1916 D17, nicknamed "Dinnaken"(*don't know*), was advancing the mile and a half to the village of Flers in support of 41st Infantry Division. Commanded by Lt. Stuart Hastie the tank was manoeuvred across crumbling support trenches and pressed on across no-man's-land, alone. Beneath a heavy barrage the tail wheels were damaged and steering became increasingly difficult. Roy managed to fire his 6-pounder gun and claimed a direct hit on a German observational balloon that was spotting for their artillery.

D17 reached Flers accompanied by infantrymen who were much reduced from enemy fire. The tank flattened a path through the heavily wired entanglement on the outskirts of the village and rolled on while about 300 soldiers moved house to house under continuing fire while D17 attempted to dislodge snipers in the buildings. After further destruction of enemy machine gun positions the tank withdrew under heavy shelling. The engine failed soon afterwards and one of the tracks took a direct hit. The crew managed to bail out and eventually returned to base.

D17, the first tank to trundle into battle, had rolled into the pages of history. The Press went crazy with stories of "a tank walking up the High Street of Flers", "Battle Cars charge trenches", "New Forts on wheels" and "His Majesty's Land Navy". The Germans called them "The Devil's Chariots." For his part Gunner Roy Reiffer was awarded the Military Medal (MM) and was later promoted to Corporal Instructor.

D17 - Dinnaken - the first attack tank

A brief biography of Roy's early years

Born in 1896 Roy was destined to share his father's joy in "tinkering with motors", starting with the family's three-wheeler Leon Bollee in 1902 and continuing with many other "infernal machines" over the years. He learned to drive a 7/9hp Chater-Lea-Jap motor cycle and sidecar and obtained his driving licence in 1910 at the age of 14.

On his 19th birthday he joined the Motor Machine Gun Corps at Bisley and within weeks volunteered for a hush-hush job on the British secret weapon – the Tank.

After the Flers incident Roy saw further front-line action until his tank "collected" a shell in the forward starboard petrol tank. Half the crew were killed and 30,000 rounds of .303 ammunition set on fire.

In 1917 he was moved to the First Tank Driving School in France to instruct the new Battalions sent out from Bovington Camp. He returned to Dorset in 1918 and stayed on after the Armistice to get demobbed, buying a private hire and taxi business with a friend, plying their trade mainly between Wool Station and Bovington Camp.

Later they managed to secure a lease on some land but before their planned lock-up garages were built Roy's partner died of TB.

The first five lock-ups were completed in 1922 and a Private Shaw, rolling up one afternoon on a Brough Superior motorcycle and sidecar, was the first taker of one, paying 2/6 a week rent. He proved to be a very good customer and was, of course,...

Lawrence of Arabia

Having to maintain the Brough and supply tyres, petrol, oil and other accessories meant Roy had "carte blanche use of the motorcycle"

Early in 1923 Lawrence had lent Roy the Brough and sidecar for a Sunday run-out with his fiancée Nora. They decided to go to Devon to see friends but ran out of petrol approaching Honiton. When coasting down the hill into town a motorcyclist shot out from a side road, collided with the Brough and damaged the petrol tank and oil drip-feed installation. Lawrence was sympathetic and told Roy to send the damaged parts to the manufacturer George Brough and have the bill sent to him. Roy refused and subsequently paid the £10.15.8 himself but never forgot Lawrence's generosity.

During the winter, because of a fuel shortage at the camp, Lawrence decided to launch a clandestine but successful coal scrounging escapade "for the boys". The sort of hi-jinks typical of the man.

By now a repair shop had been built and a Shell petrol pump installed. The Red Garage at Bovington was up and running.

In 1924 Lawrence arrived on a new SS80 Brough, having travelled from the North of England, and was not happy having been booked at Bere Regis, just four miles away, for a noisy exhaust.

In the same year Lawrence ordered a new lightweight Francis-Burnett from Roy at a cost of £35 for use on short journeys. This was very useful, but only until a soldier "borrowed" it as a prank and drove it over the edge of a gravel quarry. Scarcely two

Roy Reiffer on Lawrence of Arabia's SS80 Brough Superior in 1924

months old the motorcycle was badly bent and buckled. Lawrence said he didn't want to see the bike again and anyone could have the wreck for £5. Roy bought it!

At times Lawrence would ask Roy to look after fairly large amounts of cash for him (£50 was a lot in the 1920s), to put against his accounts and with the knowledge that he could always get a "fiver" if he needed to. Roy said Lawrence never counted it out and refused to take a receipt. He said the money was his wages as a private soldier.

Lawrence was unable to attend Roy's wedding at St. Christopher's Church, Winfrith, on 11 April 1925, but gave £5 for a wedding present and accepted an invitation to tea to meet "the bride" at her parent's home. He roared into the yard at East Farm, Winfrith, one Sunday, was introduced to Nora Chick Gould and her parents and entertained the family over tea with an interesting conversation about the Royal Family. He left and went on to visit Theodore Powys, the writer, at East Chaldon, a village about two miles away. Lawrence later lent Roy and Nora his Brough and sidecar for their honeymoon in Cornwall.

During this time he used to "breeze" into the garage quite a lot and Roy remembers him saying one hot day that he was off for a dip at Lands End ! Another time he rode to Canterbury for an unscheduled meeting with Archbishop Lang because he thought it an injustice for soldiers to be forced to attend compulsory church parades.

On one occasion when requiring a day off the Company Officer at Bovington turned down Lawrence's request. The next day a telegram arrived "Release Pte. Shaw immediately !" signed by Winston Churchill.

Enter Don Reiffer as an infant

Don Reiffer was born at Moreton in April 1930, the second of three sons to Roy and Nora. His earliest memories recall visits to the Red Garage by Lawrence who would pick him up, sit him astride the petrol tank and give him rides on his motorbike. At this time the Reiffers lived in a railway carriage behind the Garage.

Lawrence, over the years, had several new Broughs and was very particular about their maintenance. He was a fast rider and Roy, who rode them all, found they handled very well at speeds over 60mph but were top heavy with a tendency for a front wheel skid to develop at low speeds.

On the morning of the fateful day in May 1935 when he crashed, Lawrence called into the Red Garage and Roy served him with petrol while he sat astride his SS.100 Brough-Superior. He paid, kick-started the machine and was off through the Camp towards Clouds Hill. Minutes later the accident occurred. He never regained consciousness and died in Bovington Military Hospital, just opposite the Garage. Later his Brough was taken back to the Garage and placed at the back of the petrol pump from which it had last been filled up.

Roy Reiffer had known Lawrence for over 12 years and rated him a real gentleman who despised money and position and was a great supporter of the underdog. At the time of Lawrence's death the Reiffers were living at Sunnymede, Broadmayne.

The end of an era

The next year young Donald was staying with his paternal grandparents at Cranmer House, just off the Old Kent Road, when through the window of his bedroom at the top of the house he watched Crystal Palace destroyed in a spectacular fire. It was

The Crystal Palace fire in 1936

the night of November 30, 1936 and the New York Times front page reported "Engulfed in a roaring sheet of flames, which towered so high into the night sky that it could be seen almost from the English Channel, the world famous Crystal Palace, architectural pride of the Victorian era, crashed to earth – a raging inferno of twisted girders and molten glass." Sir Winston Churchill called it "the end of an era."

In 1939 Roy was still running the Red Garage and, with his family, living at Broadmayne. When war was declared, being unable to get fuel because of a Government ban – only about one in seven garages were allowed to supply petrol – the business was forced to close. Now in his 40s Roy was recruited as an engineer, moved near Gloucester, and worked in a top secret aircraft factory, under Frank Whittle who was researching jet propulsion. Roy made component parts for the first jet engine to be flown successfully in a Gloster aircraft in 1941.

Don at this time was sent to Hampton Grammar School at Glasbury near Hay-on-Wye where, he says, he received a good "commonsense" education. The family had moved to Llyswen nearby and to "Green Pit", a large house in three acres with frontage and fishing rights to the River Wye.

With the war over and being able to sell petrol once more a brief return to Dorset lead to the Red Garage being sold to Jacobs of Bedford. Don left school in 1946 and became an apprenticed motor mechanic in Glasbury, deferring National Service.

Enter the swing era

His mother Nora played the piano and she had always encouraged her three sons to take up music. With friends they started a seven piece dance band and were soon booked to play at local hops and dance halls. It was at one of these 'do's', in 1948 at Talgarth, that Don met his future wife Margaret. They started courting and became engaged just before she started a nursing career at Hereford County Hospital and he joined the RAF to do his National Service in 1951.

Don escaped most of the routine military training because of his prowess on the alto sax and clarinet. He was in demand to play in various RAF Station Bands and quickly passed his RAF driving test in the single decker bus that he subsequently used for ferrying the bands about. He was successful as well in mechanical trade training and achieved the coveted Certificate of Merit AOC.

Don and Margaret were married at Talgarth in August 1953, just two months before Don completed his National Service. They celebrated their Diamond Wedding Anniversary last year, having had four children - Susan, Martin, Jane and Tony - and 18 different addresses. Over the years they became well known in South Dorset. They moved to Weymouth in 1967 when Don was offered the managership of Currys in Yeovil, having worked for the firm in Port Talbot and Newbury.

This was followed by managerial spells with Cecil Hadley Electrical near Weymouth Bridge, Rogers & Dawes Electrical next to the County Museum in Dorchester and shop manager for the Electrical, Gardening and Kitchenware Departments of Debenhams in separate premises in St. Mary Street, Weymouth.

Roy and Nora Reiffer in 1963

Roy Reiffer came back to Weymouth where he died in 1970, but not before seeing Don and Margaret set up business for themselves in a Waterloo Place Guest House. This was followed by the purchase of a larger seafront hotel and then in 1980 The Kingswood Hotel in Rodwell.

A change of direction lead to the opening of a specialist delicatessen in Dorchester. The "Country Stile" in the Hardye Arcade, off South Street, was the Reiffer's pride and joy for 13 years until retirement in 1997. Don's mother, Nora, died in 1990 at the age of 86.

From an extended trip to The Festival of Britain in 1951, visiting Ronnie Scott's Jazz Club to see all time hero Freddy Gardner play alto sax with the Peter Yorke Orchestra and to have a professional session on Don's own instruments, with Continental holidays won in the 1960s as prizes when working as a rep for Hoover, champagne trips to London and the Epsom Derby and, later, to traipsing around the British countryside towing their own caravan, Don and Margaret have lived life to the full.

Although currently not enjoying the best of health - Margaret having suffered a stroke and Don having undergone a multi-by-pass heart operation in the past few years - Don has one ambition left. He is desperate to find the whereabouts of and acquire his father's wartime medals so that he can donate them to the Bovington Tank Museum; where he knows they will be preserved for the Nation along with the story of

Dinnaken and will be available for the ever expanding Reiffer generations to visit and muse on the life and times of their remarkable forefather.

Many locals in Weymouth and Dorchester will remember Don and Margaret Reiffer from this picture taken in the 1980s

It's there for us – AGE UK (Dorchester)

Getting older and needing help? Make a call says Trevor Vacher-Dean

Age UK - IT Manager, Jane Askew, teaching one-to-one computing

IT may not be the answer to all your problems but I bet this local charity can help. AGE UK is for all of us as we grow older.

Offering support and services (many of them FREE) for the over 50s, the clear objective of AGE UK (Dorchester) is to make a real difference to the lives of older people in Dorset. And it does just that in many diverse ways.

Whether you need advice, access to services or are looking for a bit of local fun, this is for you.

AGE UK (Dorchester) is governed by trustees, and is one of 160 nationwide, independent charities under the umbrella of AGE UK; formed in 2009 by the merging of AGE CONCERN and HELP THE AGED to become the UK's largest charity for older people.

This organisation, now in its third year, ensures that all money raised locally by the services, activities and the two AGE UK charity shops (in Dorchester and on Portland) is spent across the whole of 'rural' Dorset. AGE UK (Bournemouth) has a similar operation for the county's eastern conurbation.

Promoting the well-being of older people

AGE UK aims to enrich the experience of older people to make later life more enjoyable and fulfilling by providing direct and practical ways to facilitate

Rowan Cottage, Dorchester

independence and alleviate anxiety with support information and advice on benefits, health, disability and the provision of many other services.

Operating from headquarters at Rowan Cottage in the County Town, AGE UK offers care provision at its Day Centre or through its home support service which offers help with many domestic issues including cleaning, washing and ironing, shopping, gardening, paperwork and even dog walking. Their Reach-Out Service helps older isolated people to get out more, meet new people and be more active. There are lunch clubs, exercise classes, computer courses, social activities and day trips, a gardening club, art classes and talks.

Other facilities on offer include toe nail cutting and foot care, specialist over 50s insurance, a minibus shopping service and occasional classes in foreign languages, cryptic crosswords and sessions on music and games. There are also FREE surgeries on making wills, powers of attorney and other legal aspects of home and finance.

Memory Advisory Service

AGE UK Dorchester, with AGE UK Bournemouth, under contract to Dorset County Council and NHS Dorset, delivers the Memory Advisory Service which provides comprehensive support for people with memory loss and their carers. On the basis "that no-one should go through memory loss or dementia alone" the service employs 14 staff across Dorset to help the "many people with memory loss, and their families, face a challenging future."

AGE UK is a remarkable organisation, supported by an army of volunteers. It is there to help those who have everything as well as those who have nothing.

One of the most thoughtful and precious gifts to give to an "oldie", even those who supposedly "want for nothing", is the following information.

AGE UK (Dorchester)
Rowan Cottage
4 Prince of Wales Road
Dorchester
DT1 1PW

Phone: 01305 269444
www.ageuk.org.uk/dorchester

AGE UK(Bournemouth)
700 Wimborne Road
Winton
Bournemouth
BH9 2EG

Phone: 01202 530530
www.ageuk.org.uk/bournemouth

Without the one-to-one computer lessons arranged for me by Age UK (Dorchester) with volunteer trainer Bob Reynolds I, technologically an old dinosaur, would have been unable to accept the appointment as Year Book Editor. I am naturally very grateful to this wonderful charity.

The MV Freedom

and everything you should know about it by Patrick Dowding-Vesey

MV Freedom at Durdle Door

MV Freedom is a Blythe 33 motor catamaran adapted for the disabled and can carry up to 12 passengers – including up to six wheelchairs, a skipper and two crew. MV Freedom is a registered charity and welcomes people of all ages.

In 1982 the Acorns Day Centre conceived the idea of purchasing a boat that would provide a unique service for the benefit and enjoyment of people with a disability, the elderly and those with learning difficulties.

In 1984 'Friends of the MV Freedom' charity was formed to buy a boat and the first MV Freedom was purchased for £25000. It was in service for ten years until safety standards were tightened, leading to the purchase of the current boat in 1994 at a cost of £52000. Further funds were spent to upgrade the boat and adapt the equipment on board to enable full wheelchair access and comply with the Maritime and Coastguard Agency new regulations. In the winter of 2011/12 Freedom's wheelhouse was extended to cover most of the open deck to provide much welcomed protection from spray and the elements, converting Freedom into a more all-weather boat and thereby enabling us to extend the running season and cancel fewer trips should the weather become inclement.

The MV Freedom crew

We get paid in smiles

The Officers, Skippers, Crew and friends are all volunteers and give their time freely. They say 'we get paid in smiles'.

MV Freedom provides the opportunity for our passengers to enjoy the beautiful Jurassic coast from a seaward perspective and spend a few hours out at sea. Many Day Centres and Care Homes from Dorset, and surrounding counties, regularly benefit from the service we provide which is also available to disabled groups and individuals holidaying in the area.

Trips on MV Freedom start from our convenient and easily accessible mooring on the North Quay pontoon. We pass under the Town bridge and enjoy views of Weymouth's historic harbour. Continuing seaward, we pass the RNLI lifeboat the

'Ernest and Mable', the Condor ferry and the Victorian sea-defences of the 'Nothe Fort' before leaving the harbour and entering Weymouth Bay.

Depending on tides, sea state, weather and time allowed, Freedom normally heads east along the stunning Jurassic coast to Durdle Door and on to Lulworth Cove where we anchor for lunch before returning home. If conditions are not favourable, our alternative trip takes us to Portland Harbour, the venue for the 2012 Olympic and Paralympics sailing events. Portland harbour's historic features are of particular interest to those visiting the area, especially the many war veterans who have joined us on these trips.

Fishing rods are available on board for those who wish to do some very casual fishing. We work a 'buddy' system allowing anyone the opportunity to fish, much to the delight of those who had always thought they would not be able to experience the thrill of being at sea let alone catch their own dinner. Our passengers are also welcome to helm the boat when the skipper considers it safe to do so and this provides a great deal of joy and pleasure to both passengers and crew. One member of our crew recalls a young girl who could not see over the wheel let alone through the window but the pleasure and excitement showing on her face was the highlight of his day and indeed has remained one of his best memories during his time crewing on Freedom. Another memory is that of a boy, who could only communicate by hitting and kicking, seen laying across the bench with his head on his carer's lap and smiling for the first time anyone could remember.

The Paralympic Flame

MV Freedom gets involved with other charities and events. We often act as committee boat or mother ship for national and local sailing activities. On Monday 27th August 2012 we were very proud to be asked to carry the Paralympic flame from Portland into Weymouth. We welcomed the ambassador and flame on board, sailed around Weymouth Bay before entering the harbour where we were greeted by hundreds of people, including local dignitaries, camera crews and photographers.

Since it's inception in 1984, the Friends of freedom charity has become well established and gained tremendous support from local businesses, dignitaries and individuals who help with the crucial fund raising needed to keep the boat running whether it be financially or by providing equipment, victuals, raffle prizes, venues and assistance with administration, organisation and running of events and activities. Clearly, without this support MV Freedom would be unable to function. The cost of running and maintaining the boat is considerable with fuel alone costing around £5,000 a year, plus up to another £10,000 each year for winter refit, safety equipment, MCA inspections, running maintenance and repairs, together with mandatory licences. This figure would be considerably higher were it not for the generosity of Dean & Readyhof who lift Freedom out each year and clean her bottom before taking her to Sunseekers who generously deal with any required hull maintenance or damage repairs. The team, with the help of our ship's engineer Danny Shuttle, then carry out all other required work to make her Shipshape-and-Bristol-Fashion for the spring.

Fund raising at Abbotsbury and on Dartmoor

The two major fund raising events which currently take place annually are the Swannery Walk and the Dartmoor barrel challenge. The Swannery walk is held in June when the management of Abbotsbury Swannery allows us free access. Participants consist of clients, their relatives and carers from local care homes who obtain sponsors for completing a trip around the Abbotsbury Swannery. On completion of the route, most partake of a picnic lunch whilst taking in the fresh sea air and enjoying the wonderful scenery. Clearly, a great deal of pleasure is gained from this activity as many return to participate year after year.

MV Freedom passing under Weymouth Bridge

The Dartmoor Barrel Challenge is held in September and for this more arduous event we team up with "Help for Heroes". Across the country, teams are formed and sponsored for completing the task of transporting a beer barrel approximately 15 miles across the unforgiving terrain of Dartmoor, culminating with a fun barrel roll in fancy dress along the Harbour side in Weymouth.

The teams arrive to set up camp on Dartmoor on Friday, complete the task on Saturday, and on Sunday, descend on Weymouth Harbour to roll their barrel from Hope Square to the Kings Arms. A shield is awarded to the team, judged by the local MP (currently Richard Drax) to have the most imagination. This is followed by fun and entertainment in the Kings Arms.

MV Freedom has been operating in her current role for 19 years and was a fishing boat prior to this. Although she is still sound and very seaworthy it is costing more each year to keep her fit for purpose.

Four years ago a new boat fund was set up, with boat drawings produced and estimates obtained. Unfortunately, due to the current economic situation, our plans for purchasing a new boat have been put temporarily on hold. However, with the ongoing and continued generosity of our supporters, we are confident our dream of purchasing a new boat will come to fruition.

In the meantime we will continue to provide the much valued and beneficial service with our current MV Freedom.

Foggy morning, poppies in the Piddle Valley by Andrew Hepburn

Portland Sheep by Andrew Hepburn

Golden Cap from Chesil Beach by Andrew Hepburn

Bridge at Briantspuddle by Andrew Hepburn

Robbing Time is a Heinous Crime

by Hayne Russell

IT'S Market Day in Dorchester and there is a large gathering of farmers and dealers in the Antelope Hotel. Gradually, as the drink takes hold the conversation becomes more ribald and heated and before long many are "Dree sheets t' the wind". One farmer from the other side of Sydling suddenly announces " Best be on whome vor tis dark coz dozen want nar b......robbin I ". This was met with hoots of laughter from the gathering and one remarked "Gid on wi' 'ee Bert, these got nothin worth pinchin" "Ah" comes the response, "Thas what thee d' think" and with that he took a handful of sovereigns from his pocket followed by a large gold watch. "I did zum good business today and thick watch bin in me vamily ver yers. Mean a lot t'I" He then opened the back of the watch and showed the initials "A J.P." " 'Longed to me vather zee". He remained a short while longer, but the assembled group failed to notice a couple of men who had been at the bar suddenly drink up and hurriedly leave. Bert finally bid good day and left.

After collecting his horse he made his way down The Grove, out through Stratton and on to Sydling. By the time he reached the ford at the end of Sydling it was just getting dark and he failed to see the wire which had been stretched across just under the surface of the water. As he entered the ford his horse stumbled. Bert was thrown from the saddle and hit the ground with enough force to stun him. He was too weak to resist two figures who suddenly appeared and roughly searched his pockets. It was over very quickly and by the time he had staggered to his feet they had fled with his sovereigns and watch. His horse, although standing nearby, was slightly lame so he made his way home on foot, in a very sorry state.

Later of course, the village Constable was on the case but a serious matter such as a robbery would have involved someone from the newly formed detective branch. The enquiries proved fruitless.

A timely set up

Some months later a detective officer known for his prodigious memory was quietly sitting in the corner of a bar at Maiden Newton mulling over the difficulties he was facing in convincing his uniform colleagues that there was a need for plain clothes officers. It was proving an up-hill battle with even senior officers clearly showing that they had no time for such nonsense!

There was a group of customers at the bar and he heard one remark to the landlord "Yer, landlord thick clock o' thine be vive minutes zlow". The landlord looked up at the clock on the wall and said" Never, thick clock bin in me vamily ver sixty yers an' never lost a minute". To which the questioner said "Well, I bet thee a pound thick clock be zlow".

The detective who had been quietly listening to this repartee, responded immediately. He got to his feet and said "You'm on zunner" and slapped a pound note on the counter. The questioner surprised at this stranger's sudden intervention, slowly removed a large gold watch from his pocket and held it up for all to see and said "I told 'ee zo, this yer watch be always right". The detective leant across and grabbed his arm and said "Well now me zunner jist open up thick watch ver I a minute". Thinking that he had made himself an easy pound and with nothing to fear he opened up the back of the watch and there for all to see were the initials "A.J.P".

The detective who had for some time suspected that this man had had some connection with the robbery, knowing that he was a regular drinker in the pub, decided to set up this little charade with the help of the landlord who had deliberately altered his clock. The detective hoped that this might cause the gold watch to be produced and as it turned out his luck was in.

One arrest for the new detective branch and Bert would get his watch back.

Thomas Hardy and All That

Brenda Parry gives her report on The Hardy Society

THOMAS Hardy, Dorchester, Dorset and Wessex form the hub of the Thomas Hardy Society with the author, whom we consider to be the greatest 19th century novelist and the finest 20th century poet, at the very heart of all our activities. But were it not for the Dorset environment it's quite possible our writer would never have existed.

So taking on Thomas Hardy we take on all that entails; the beauty of the Dorset countryside, the character of Dorset towns and villages and the people that go to make up those communities.

2013 was one of the busiest years for a very long time despite it not being a conference year. It marked the 140th anniversary of the publication of 'A Pair of Blue Eyes', the 135th of 'The Return of the Native' and the 125th of 'Wessex Tales' and it was November 2012 that marked the death of Emma, Hardy's first wife.

All these events we celebrated or commemorated, but it has been "behind the scenes" that so much activity has taken place this year.

Fight against houses plan and local wind farm

Nobody was more horrified than the Thomas Hardy Society when Dorset Council proposed to build 1,000 houses on Came Down, the beautiful cornfields and agricultural land overlooked by Hardy's home at Max Gate and through which Hardy would walk to William Barnes'Came Rectory. With support of the William Barnes Society, the National Trust and many outraged local residents we shouted long and hard until our cries were taken up by the Daily Mail and The Times.

Leading the battle and giving much weight to our arguments, our president and currently Dorset's favourite man, Lord Fellowes, made his opposition to the scheme quite clear. Most of Came Down is owned by the Duchy of Cornwall and during the weeks of the campaign the Prince of Wales appeared on television to reiterate his love for the countryside and to urge us all to nurture it. The papers had a bit of a field day and the council backed down, for the time being at least. And we like to think the Prince, himself, was opposed to such a plan.

We have also protested about the proposed wind farm near Puddletown which could seriously affect the wonderful vistas across Egdon Heath. We keep an eye on the environment and anything that could spoil the world that Hardy so loved and immortalised in both verse and prose, and which we continue to enjoy today.

Back to the man and his family

We started the year with a visit to St. Juliot in Cornwall where Hardy and Emma first met. Some members were lucky enough to stay in the Old Rectory, currently run as a stylish bed and breakfast establishment by Hardy enthusiasts, Chris and Sally Searle. It was here where Emma had lived with her sister and brother-in-law, the then Rector of St. Juliot. Hardy was sent there as a young architect to advise on the state of the church but his memories of that visit 'When I set off for Lyonesse…..' were far more concerned with the young girl who rode her pony along the cliff tops than of any architectural plans. For us the March visit proved to be a wonderful weekend of poetry and walks in the footsteps of the poet accompanied by the 21st century award winning poet Christopher Reid, who like Hardy wrote movingly of his own wife's death.

With the remarkable love poems of 1912/1913, generally considered to be some of Hardy's finest work, very much in our thoughts, so, too, of course, was their subject Emma. The anniversary of her November 1912 death was commemorated with a wreath-laying at Stinsford Church which had been preceded with a weekend of poetry and talks in her memory at Max Gate.

Hardy's marriage to Emma lasted nearly forty years and as we have said inspired some of his most beautiful poems, and so the THS took celebrations of her life very seriously. In April there was an outing to Plymouth from whence Emma's family came and where she had spent most of her childhood.

Hardy's Cottage and Max Gate

But let's go backstage again. All sorts of things have been happening in Bockhampton at Hardy's Cottage and at Max gate, the home in Dorchester which he designed himself. Both properties are now owned by the National Trust. The interior of Max Gate has been transformed inside to look almost as it did in Hardy's lifetime, and it has become not only a popular tourist venue but a regular staging post for THS events and many other cultural activities. And to add to the charm, the inimitable musician, Tim Laycock, is frequently to be found playing his squeeze box and talking to visitors about Hardy's Dorset. He also plays at the cottage - all thanks to the National Trust, and to the delight of visitors.

The birthplace hidden away in Thorncomb Wood, on the edge of Hardy's Egdon Heath, is to get an impressive visitor centre as a result of the Hardy County Project, towards which the THS has obtained a £50.000 grant of charitable funds for interpretive facilities in the centre and on the heath.

The Old Rectory at St. Juliot in Cornwall, a century after Hardy met Emma there.

And to our delight once again animals , cattle and horses, are being allowed to graze the heath in order to return it to the state it was in, in Hardy's day.

One way and another, the council of management, under the chairmanship of Dr. Tony Fincham, has had little pause for breath in recent months.

Hardy's Birthday at the beginning of June was celebrated in traditional style with a walk round upper and lower Bockhampton led by Derek Pride who was born and grew up in the village.

A challenging birthday lecture on Hardy's relationship with Robert Browning was delivered by Dr. Alan Chedzoy, chairman of the William Barnes Society. This was followed by readings from the New Hardy Players and then the ceremonial wreath-laying on the Hardy statue at the Top o' Town, followed by another wreath being laid on William Barnes statue.

Celebrations went on throughout the evening, and continued during the early part of June in conjunction with the National Trust, Dorset County Museum, University of Exeter, Dorset Area of Outstanding Natural Beauty Partnership, Kingston Maurward College and Stinsford Parish Church, all of whom have agreed to co-ordinate activities by 2015.

September brought the annual meeting and for once it was not held in Dorchester, but at the Acorn Inn at Evershot, in the heart of Woodlanders country. This began with an amazing walk through George Melbury's and Giles Winterbourne's woodlands led by the deer-keeper, Richard Squires.

And after the business of the day and supper, readings from the Woodlanders followed by our very own readers in residence, Furze Swann and Sue Theobald.

Society Members on Rainbarrow where they lit the "Return of the Native" bonfire.

The Bishop of Wakefield, bonfire at Rainbarrow and Mellstock Quire

One of the highlights of our year, came in October with the Bishop of Wakefield, the Rt Rev Stephen Platt delivering the London lecture and spelling out very clearly the difference in his understanding of Hardy from that of his predecessor, Bishop Walsham How of Wakefield who was so horrified by the content of 'Jude the Obscure', he threw the novel on the fire, much to Hardy's distress. It has been suggested that this incident persuaded Hardy to stop writing novels and return to his first love, poetry. It may have contributed but there were many other reasons.

The standing room only lecture at Birkbeck College received a standing ovation in every sense of the word. Many said afterwards that it was the best lecture on Hardy's tortuous relationship with religion they had ever heard.

The next highlight, quite literally, was the lighting of a bonfire on Rainbarrow to mark the 135th anniversary of the publication of the Return of the Native. What a vision, but Eustacia Vye was nowhere to be found and Napoleon did not invade.

And for the first time, 'Going the Rounds' in the footsteps of the Mellstock Quire on Christmas Eve (we did it on December 21) was led by Tim Laycock, Mike Bailey and 'The Madding Crowd' accompanied by Furze Swann, who had done such sterling service leading the event over the years. But Furze was still there ensuring the continuity of this favourite event.

It has been a good year for the THS, but there's an open invitation for you to join us in the future. This year we have our *International Conference* in Dorchester, at the end of July, when Hardy aficionados from all over the world join us for some amazing lectures, and walks to places they never knew existed. Should you feel you know Dorset all too well, then join us in Oxford when the poet laureate, Carol Ann Duffy will be our main speaker during the weekend of March 29.

Long may all Dorset men and women celebrate the life of its most famous son, Thomas Hardy.

To join the THS go to our website www.hardysociety.org or email at info@ hardysociety.org. We look forward to hearing from you.

. . . .

YOU OLDIES CAN'T WRITE...LIKE...INNIT!!

My grandson, on flicking through the pages of a recent Year Book, said there was too much punctuation and that at school he is discouraged from using commas. This sentence is therefore dedicated to him:

Since retiring my wife occupies her time with cooking the grandchildren and the local council and enjoys shooting dogs and Bruce Forsyth.

So, young man, put that in your exercise book and show it to your teacher. *The Editor.*

Paranormal Purbeck

A study of the unexplained by David Leadbetter

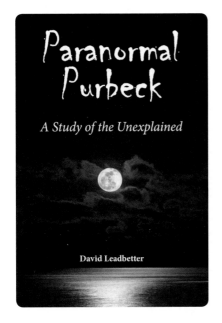

GHOSTS galore, footsteps echoing from the past, objects moving of their own volition, near death experiences, displacements in time, memories from the future, UFO sightings, synchronicities....this book is a collection of remarkable experiences from the Isle of Purbeck, writes Roving Press publisher Julie Musk.

Most of the first- hand accounts have never been published before, and suggest that what is termed "paranormal" is more commonplace than generally supposed and is perceived intuitively, depending on the right combination of circumstances.

Anyone with a thirst for mysteries and a desire to extend the frontiers of human knowledge will be gripped. The author challenges fixed opinions and beliefs, offering detailed personal experiences from a small geographical area and arguing that we need a fundamental reappraisal of how we view the world.

David Leadbetter's "intriguing look at the world"

Mention the word "paranormal" and it will evoke different responses from different people: for those of a particular religious persuasion it may arouse suspicion or hostility, while for some who may be very rational in nature, it may lead to ridicule or scepticism. The majority of open-minded people, however, accept that paranormal phenomena occur, even if they are not sure what exactly they are, or how they are caused.

In his introduction to *Paranormal Purbeck* David argues that there are two ways of looking at the world: a narrow view, blinkered through dogma, prejudice and

Author and ghost hunter
David Leadbetter

preconceived notions and a wider vision that takes into account such inexplicable phenomena as ghosts, poltergeists, precognition, telepathy, near death experiences and UFO sightings. He suggests that we perceive the paranormal through the intuitive side of our brain – the same side that artists, musicians and writers use to produce their work.

David became interested in the subject as a boy and it became clear to him that paranormal phenomena are widespread and experienced by a large number of people, as is shown by the many accounts collected by the Society for Psychical Research since the 19th century.

Esoteric theoretical physics

"I was fascinated by the ways in which the paranormal might connect with certain aspects of theoretical physics which can be fairly esoteric – parallel worlds, string theory, quantum mechanics, relativity, dark matter and dark energy. We are discovering so

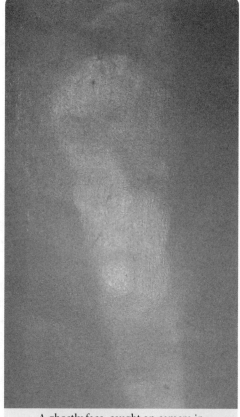

A ghostly face caught on camera in the Royal Oak by the author.

much that is new and strange about the physical world that it is highly probable that what is termed 'paranormal' relates to other worlds that may lie beyond the physical. As human beings we may be just scratching the surface." David considers a deeper understanding of the paranormal could shed light on some of the greatest mysteries, such as what happens when our bodies die?

David has spent most of his life in Swanage and was aware of the old ghost stories in Purbeck, such as the "Phantom Army" at Creech and the "Headless Woman" at Corfe, but he was interested to find out how many new stories were out there. Extensive personal research provided far more material than he had expected. Paranormal Purbeck has stories relating to nearly 70 locations in this small geographical area which illustrates that paranormal phenomena is more common than generally supposed.

Langton Matravers historian and curator of the Purbeck Stone Museum, Reg Saville, and landlady of The Royal Oak at Herston, Rachael Aplin, were enthusiastic supporters of David's research and both contributed much to the book. A whole chapter is devoted to the strange and mysterious goings on in the Royal Oak which appears to be a very seriously haunted pub.

The haunted Royal Oak at Herston, Swanage

Parochial but not provincial

The bulk of the material in Paranormal Purbeck relates to ghostly phenomena and associated poltergeist activity but there are other thought provoking chapters on *time*, with local accounts of premonitions, precognitive dreams and synchronicities, *UFO sightings* and *near death experiences* which offers evidence of a case for our survival after physical death. In the final chapter David draws the strands together and analyses some of the common elements that form the basis of paranormal experiences.

David's intention in the book is not to sensationalise but to present personal accounts in an accurate and coherent way, making an important distinction between "belief" and "experience". His view is that the case for the paranormal is overwhelming.

Without being too academic this is a serious book that is well written, easily read and entertaining. It poses enough questions to be mentally stimulating yet offers some satisfactory conclusions. Its title may be parochial but the contents are far reaching and way above the provincial.

Paranormal Purbeck is on sale locally at £9.99 - ISBN 978-1-8906651-220 – or direct from the publisher – www.rovingpress.co.uk - tel: 01300 321531.

Mrs Jane Tutton of West Bay

Allan Cooper remembers his great aunt

JANE Tutton lived at 14 The Arcade, West Bay. She was the widow of a Coastguard.

While shopping in Bridport, Jane read the name badge of a shop manager. It was Buike, her maiden name. She was too shy to discuss the name.

Jane's son Tom served all his Royal Navy career in submarines. M2 -1927; Orpheus -1930; Porpoise – 1934; Parthian – 1937; Taku – 1939; Tetrarch – 1941.

The London Gazette of 28 June 1940 listed Tom's name and award of the DSM "In recognition of daring endurance and resource in the conduct of hazardous and successful operations in His Majesty's submarines against the enemy." Tom was a Chief Coxswain.

A photo taken outside 14 The Arcade, West Bay, shows Jane with her brother Fred Buike M.V.O. (Member of Royal Victorian Order).

Jane cleaned St. Andrew's Mission Church, and rang the bell at service times. I cannot remember when she died.

SAINT ANDREW'S MISSION
-BRIDPORT- WEST BAY-

Editor's note: The drawing of St. Andrew's Mission was by O. Newbold and published in the 1931 Dorset Year Book.

Flashing Four White Every 20 Seconds

a tale of "bonjour matelot", "mal de mer" and Portland Bill Lighthouse -
by New "Fellow Dorset", Ian Brooke

MY first glimpse of Portland Bill lighthouse was at five minutes to midnight one windy summer night in 1969 as I prepared to descend to the engine room, with my bucket, on my first ever seagoing watch as a very junior engineer. As I looked over to starboard, about five miles away, there it was – the light flashing brightly four times every twenty seconds.

Some two years previously, while living in Portsmouth, I had taken a fancy to pottering about the harbour in one of those little yellow and black boats that seemed to be everywhere among the docks and Royal Navy ships. Unfortunately, it seemed only ex-RN personnel were taken on as drivers but I was told that if I worked for two years in the dockyard as a fitter I could apply to become an engineer officer with the Port Auxiliary Service.

And so I left my job in cinema management and went back to being a fitter.

PASV Kinterbury

Two years later I found myself about to go down into the engine room of the armament carrier *Kinterbury*. She was built in 1943, just one year after I was born, was only 200 feet long, had a displacement of 1500 tons and was powered by a tiny little sewing machine of a steam engine which pushed her along at a maximum speed of nine knots.

We had been tasked with delivering a cargo of "squid" anti-submarine mortar bombs to the Royal Fleet Auxiliary ship *Fort Sandusky*, which was at anchor in Barry Roads just off Cardiff. The only way we could transfer our load of high explosive was to tie up alongside the RFA ship and use her derrick to lift the squids, two at a time, from our hold and place them in hers.

There is always a problem with this sort of exercise. Two vessels tied to each other in a seaway will each move at different rates, particularly when one is only about a tenth the size of the other.

I was off watch and "goofing" on the bridge as the transfer took place. As a pair of squids came up out of the hold on the end of a rope we rolled to port as the *Fort*

Sandusky rolled to starboard. We both rolled back the opposite way just as the load cleared our hold and I watched with horror as the pair of mortar bombs, laden with high explosive, took a swing toward the towering side of the RFA ship. Seconds seemed to become hours as the squids accelerated towards the hull and I knew that I was watching my last moments tick away until, with a mighty bo-o-oing!, like J Arthur Rank's gong, they hit the plates... and bounced off, leaving a dent which looked like an enormous pair of spectacles.

The ups and downs of a disappearing ship

Our next load was of old fashioned moored mines, those with the horns, which had to be delivered to the Admiralty Mine Depot at Pembroke Dock. No trauma here, except that I had gone ashore to the Merchant Navy Club for a little liquid refreshment and when I returned to the pier the *Kinterbury* was gone!

After a pint or three, a shock like this was not good for the digestive system. I very quickly sobered up and started looking around the anchorage for my ship.

In my slightly befuddled state I had not remembered leaving the ship at high tide. At about 35 feet, the rise and fall of the tide at Pembroke Dock is one of the greatest in the British Isles. I, of course, had returned to our mooring at low tide. I soon realised, as I ran to the end of the pier, that *Kinterbury* had not sailed anywhere because, as I glanced down, I was looking straight down her funnel.

The following morning we had to go upriver to take on fuel at a floating pontoon. This was in fact a very old ship which had the fuel pipes and valves bolted to what remained of its decks. It was not until years later that I realised that I been walking on *HMS Warrior*, soon to be taken to Hartlepool to be restored to museum condition and put on display in Portsmouth's Historic Dockyard.

This trip round part of the British coast was the first of many over a sixteen year period, most of which was spent in the Naval base on Portland, towing targets for the RN, and other navies, to shoot at.

This little tale of seasickness, abject terror and maritime history started with my descent into the engine room of *PASV Kinterbury* at five minutes to midnight with bucket in hand and Portland Bill Lighthouse, flashing four white every twenty seconds, about five miles north. It finishes four hours later as I came off watch, with my bucket now containing the remains of my last night's supper, to see about five miles off the starboard beam.....yes! you have guessed it.....Portland Bill Lighthouse, flashing four white every twenty seconds, as the dawn came up astern.

Milton-on-Stour remembers one of its own

by Sam Woodcock

EVERY year on Remembrance Day we gather around Milton-on-Stour War Memorial to remember those who lost their lives in the two World Wars and other more recent conflicts. As the names are read out few if any of those listening would have known the individuals or have any idea as to the circumstances of their deaths or the devastation caused to the families they left behind. Here is a brief detail of just one.

Harry Vincent

Fred Vincent, village blacksmith, in 1956

Harry was the only son of our village blacksmith and lived with his parents Fred and Annie Vincent at the Forge in Milton. Harry attended Milton Primary School, Church and Sunday School. He was a bright boy who won a number of school prizes. In August 1905 he received the book "Martin Rattler" as "The first and best prize for scripture". The following year his prize was the book "Life on the Ocean Wave" and for Christmas in 1906 his uncle gave him the book "South Sea Whaler".

Harry was always interested in sea adventures and exploration. He studied geography and wrote on the flyleaf of his advanced English text book *"Germany ranks next to Great Britain and makes everything a country desires"*.

It was as no surprise then that, as soon as he was able, young Harry joined the Royal Navy. Perhaps he was influenced by his near neighbour and dear friend, a young man a little older than Harry who had already joined the Navy and who was later to have a distinguished career, eventually becoming a Captain.

Tragically, although he was not to know it, Harry was to be among the early casualties of the First World War, and while still in British waters and not even in armed combat. Harry had joined the battleship HMS Bulwark which, after a complete refit, was recommissioned to join the 5th Battle Squadron in June 1912. It would not have escaped Harry's notice, keen as he was on exploration, that her previous Captain in 1908 was none other than Robert Falcon Scott of Antarctic fame, who during his captaincy was the youngest junior battleship commander at the time. Was this Harry's ambition? Sadly we will never know and it was not to be.

An almighty explosion and huge loss of life

From the beginning of the First World War in August 1914, *HMS Bulwark* was assigned to the Channel Fleet based at Portland and carried out numerous patrols in the English Channel. On November 14th 1914 she, along with the 5th Battle Squadron, was transferred to Sheerness to guard against possible German invasion.

HMS Bulwark

At anchor in the estuary of the River Medway she took on board extra ammunition; a process that took several days to complete. By November 26th she was fully laden. No one is sure as to what exactly happened next. Rumours ranged from a discarded stray cigarette-end to shells being far too tightly packed, contrary to regulations, causing them to overheat, or even cordite charges being stored alongside the boiler room. Whatever the cause, witnesses from nearby ships riding at anchor reported seeing a small fire followed minutes later by an almighty explosion.

Out of a crew of 750 men, no officers and only 14 sailors survived. In terms of loss of life in any one ship in the whole of the war this catastrophe was exceeded only by the loss of the battleship *HMS Vanguard* at Scapa Flow in 1917.

The news of such a disaster befalling their only son must have been devastating to our blacksmith and his wife. Fred Vincent kept a framed portrait of his son in uniform over his mantelpiece, and on the wall next to it a framed set of three photographs of the unveiling of Milton War Memorial. These remained there until Fred's own death in 1958.

Much of this was told to me by Fred himself as an old man musing over his long and interesting life. He bequeathed to me some of Harry's school books and prizes which I treasure to this day.

· ·

BRIDPORT

"Bridport has no history". Black's Guide to Dorsetshire 1877

Sir Frederick Treves........WHO?

by Steve White

STEVE White has experienced this response from many in Dorset when talking of this famous son of the County and, in his first Dorset Year Book article, has written to set the record straight with some little known facts about the Great Man who, in 1904, became the first President of the Society of Dorset Men.

Frederick Treves was born at Cornhill, Dorchester in 1853 (a plaque on the wall of *Costa Coffee* marks the building). The young Frederick was taught by William Barnes, at his school in South Street. Barnes was to have a profound effect on Treves throughout his life. He is mentioned in 'Highways and Byways' and was often quoted by Treves, who was very fond of Barnes' poems.

Treves' father died in July 1867 and within months Frederick's mother had sold the business and moved the family to London. Here Frederick was to become a student at the Merchant Taylors School before going on to train at the London Hospital.

Treves gained fame first as the man who looked after Joseph Merrick, the Elephant Man, and secondly as Royal Surgeon to Edward VII, operating on his appendix and saving his life. Treves' actions caused the Coronation, due just two days later, to be postponed from 26th June until 9th August 1902. Considering that all heads of state from the British Empire, and other dignitaries from around the world, would already have been in London, the pressure on Treves must have been enormous, particularly as some surgeons suggested the crowning could go ahead. Treves was resolute and to Edward's outcry of "I have a Coronation on hand!" replied "It will be a funeral if you don't have the operation."

The fact that Treves was so confident with his diagnosis was not merely down to a superior medical intellect; his peers who didn't concur with his decision to operate were also leading lights of the medical profession. So what was it ?

Treves was considered one of the world's leaders in all things 'appendix' but he had made a number of poor judgments over the years; one leading to a personal tragedy.

In 1900 his 18 year-old daughter Hetty developed severe abdominal pain but Treves was sure it wasn't appendicitis. He was wrong and his hesitation to operate lead to Hetty's death through peritonitis. Treves never hesitated again and the King's life was probably saved indirectly through Hetty's untimely death.

An indebted King Edward VII commanded that the whole British Empire raise their glasses and toast Sir Frederick Treves. The Dorset lad had reached the pinnacle of his fame.

Writer, Traveller and Yachtsman

Treves had always maintained that a surgeon should retire at the age of 50 and this he did in 1903. Now a wealthy and very famous man, he decided to write travel books. The fact that almost all of them were reprinted several times proves his talent for writing. Prior to embarking on his travel book endeavours he was asked by the publishers, Macmillan & Co., to write the Dorset edition of their popular 'Highways and Byways' series. Treves accepted the challenge – and a challenge it was. He cycled over 2000 miles around the County researching his book. Here was one of the most famous people in the British Empire cycling on rough chalk tracks visiting every part of Dorset! The book was first published in 1906, was re-printed many times and still holds the title of most popular book written on Dorset.

Treves used to rent a cottage in West Lulworth and moored his yacht *'Vagabond'* in the Cove. An accomplished yachtsman, he apparently taught a number of medical colleagues to sail and even earned his Master Mariner's Certificate. He would regularly cross the English Channel single handed, even on Boxing Day. It was while staying at his cottage in Lulworth in September 1892 that a remarkable event and an astonishing coincidence took place.

A miracle at Lulworth

Treves describes it in Highways and Byways in Dorset;

"The cliffs that shut in the cove on the land side are steep and terrible. On the beach at the foot of the highest precipice is a board with this inscription on it:

This marks the spot whereon
E.H.L.
Aged 11 years
Fell from the summit of the cliff,
A descent of 380 feet.
September 7th 1892
She miraculously escaped without

Sustaining lifelong injury.

S.T.S.L.

The girl was Edith H Leckie of 1 Morningside Road, Bootle, Lancashire. Her mother, Elizabeth, was an Australian and her father an Irish Squire – hence the initials for Squire T. S. Leckie. This incident was recorded in a number of local newspapers including the Dorset County Chronicle and the Poole & Dorset Herald. Edith and her mother were visiting Lulworth Cove with friends while the Squire was in Weymouth on business. Treves continues the story;

"Any who look up from this spot to the fringe of grass which crowns this appalling wall will never for a moment credit that a child can have fallen from a height greater than that of St Paul's Cathedral without having been mangled to death. I did not actually see the poor girl fall, but I was on the beach when she was brought to the coastguard boat house, where I was able to attend to her terrible injuries. She came down with her back to the cliff. Her clothes were torn into strings, and it would appear that the catching of her garments on the rough face of the precipice, together with the circumstance that certain slopes and ledges were encountered in her descent, help to explain the incredible fact that she escaped with her life, and still more happily without permanent ill effect. Those who are curious about coincidences may be interested to know that at the time the alarm reached my cottage I was reading a book written by her father. He was himself not staying in Lulworth at the time, nor had I previously made his acquaintance."

That Treves was in Lulworth and reading a book on railway engineering by Squire T S Leckie, when the latter's daughter fell from the Lulworth cliffs is indeed a fascinating coincidence.

Sir Frederick Treves died on 7 December 1923, at the age of 70, in Lausanne, Switzerland. Ironically it was peritonitis that caused his demise which, in the days before antibiotics, commonly resulted from a ruptured appendix. Lady Frederick Treves arranged for him to be cremated at Lausanne and sent his ashes to England for burial in Dorchester cemetery. She did not attend the funeral, which took place on 2 January 1924, arranged by Sir Newman Flower, Treves' friend and publisher (and Year Book Editor from 1914-1920). The service was organised by Thomas Hardy.

Hardy, who was now 84 and very frail, was implored by Flower not to attend but he insisted.

It was bitterly cold and raining hard but Hardy stood beside the open grave, without an umbrella, for the entire ceremony. He placed a poem in *The Times* titled "In the Evening".

The Society of Dorset Men had on their wreath a verse from William Barnes, in Dorset dialect – it had been a favourite of Treves:

'An' oft do come a saddened hour
When there must go away
Woone well beloved to our heart's core
vor long, perhaps vor aye.
An' oh! It is a touchen thing
the loven heart must rue
to hear behind his last farewell
the geate a-vallen to!

Treves and Thomas Hardy had been great friends, often meeting to reminisce about old Dorset, dining on Dorset Knobs and Blue Vinny cheese, washed down with a fine Burgundy. Hardy invited funeral guests to tea and talked about Treves. He said the fact that Treves was chosen by The Society of Dorset Men as their first President, with him as the second, showed the high level of esteem in which Treves was held.

Hardy is justifiably famous and, as a son of Dorset, has probably done more to bring the County to the fore than anyone else.

Treves, conversely, is hardly known in his native county which is remarkable considering that, for a time at the beginning of the last century, he was one of the most famous men on the planet.

Diary Note: Every year, at 2.30pm on 19th April, a short memorial service to Sir Frederick Treves and William Watkins, and conducted by Society Historian and Archivist the Rev. Dr. John Travell, is held at their gravesides in Dorchester Cemetery. All are welcome to attend. **Editor.**

. . . .

THE POOLE FISH-POOL

From the position of this town on a labyrinth of creeks, it afforded convenient shelter in former times to a number of very questionable characters, who obtained a living from the sea or by other modes than lawful commerce or fishing. Hence it acquired a considerable notoriety, and became the subject of the following doggerel:

"If Poole was a fish-pool, and the men of Poole fish,
There'd be a pool for the devil, and fish for his dish."

from 'A Handbook for Residents and Travellers in Wilts and Dorset' (1856)

.......but the greatest of these is Charity

(I Corinthians 13:13)

The Society of Dorset Men – Charity Sub-Committee Report

by Andrew Prowse

THE Society of Dorset Men was founded on 7 July 1904. The Society has a long and rich history.

The four objects of The Society of Dorset Men are: "to make and to renew personal friendships and associations, to promote good fellowship among Dorset men wherever they may reside, to foster love of the county and pride in its history and traditions and to assist, by every means in its power, natives of Dorset who may stand in need of the influence and help of the Society."

In order to advance the latter of these objectives it was proposed in 2009 to form a charity subcommittee with a view to give some tangible side to this noble objective.

The proposal was first discussed at the committee meeting held on Friday 27th March 2009 and it was agreed that a subcommittee be formed consisting of the Vice Chairman, Andrew Prowse, the Treasurer, Ian Morton, and committee members Sam Woodcock and former treasurer John Rousell. Then, at the next committee meeting held on Friday 10th July 2009, discussion took place on the "proposals paper" which had been prepared and circulated with various recommendations.

Charity Policy principles were agreed as follows:-

1. Charity should be for the benefit of Dorset
2. Be of direct benefit to the people of Dorset
3. Be non political
4. Support people, culture, sport or education
5. Priority should be given to youth based charities
6. Set up an initial fund of £5,000 for charity donations
7. Add each year a sum to be decided by the committee
8. Additional fund raising at special Society events
9. Committee to decide one main charity supported each year OR a number of smaller ones
10. Could invite a speaker to attend Society functions on behalf of charity supported.
11. Committee to vote on favourite charity options.

One of our first donations was in 2010, it was £500 to the Friends of Guiding on Brownsea Island to assist in the purchase of an electric buggy to assist the disabled to access this wonderful natural jewel in Poole Harbour.

Vice Chairman Andrew Prowse [left] presents the £500 cheque to Simon Taylor, Chief Executive of the Bournemouth Symphony Orchestra. Behind are [left to right] Rob Harris [French horn,] Jenni Curiel [violin,] Kevin Morgan [trombone,] Alastair Marshallsay [percussion,] Bob Walker [basoon.] Photograph by Michel Hooper-Immins.

2011 saw us venture into the Arts and donate £500 to the Bournemouth Symphony Orchestra to assist funding of the orchestras musicians travelling to schools in Dorset to enrich and enhance the children's lives with an appreciation of good music.

One of the most popular appeals on our charity was the donation of £500 to the digital mammography machine at Dorset County Hospital which would replace outmoded x-ray equipment with a state of the art digital machine.

The Vice Chairman has the happy task of travelling around the County giving out the cheques and seeing the grateful smiles on the faces of the recipients. In 2012 the giving went on unabated and, keeping within our priority on youth, we donated £350 to the Dorset Youth Association, based in Dorchester, who help and advise local young people who are in difficulties.

Again with youth in mind the Society gave £350 to the Tornadoes of South Dorset Swimming Club which teaches around 200 local children to swim.

Vice Chairman Andy Prowse [second left] presents the cheque to Appeal Chairman Wendy Nightingale and Chief Executive Jean O'Callaghan [right.] Newsletter Editor Michel Hooper-Immins is far left. Photograph by Susie Palmer DCHFT.

[Left to right:] Miles Martin [Youth Volunteer], Ashley Bradshaw [Youth Volunteer], Andy Prowse [Vice Chairman], Tony Armstrong [Volunteer Development], Val Morton (Hon. Treasurer DYA), Rosie Cullum [Youth Worker]. Edward Trist [Youth Volunteer], Jenny Palmer [Youth Volunteer], Lorna Johnson [Project Worker], Dave Thompson [DYA Director]. Photograph by Michel Hooper-Immins.

[Left to right:] Andy Prowse [Vice Chairman] with Tornadoes' coaches Paul Dashwood, Miki
Dashwood and Amy Osment.
Photograph by Michel Hooper-Immins.

Vice Chairman Andrew Prowse [left] presents the cheque to Pam Govier and Brian Willett
[right] from the Will Mackaness Trust. Photograph by Michel Hooper-Immins.

The Society has supported the Will Mackaness Trust which helps local young people to participate in water based activities. Interestingly, rather than investing in costly equipment, the Trust uses existing qualified providers. The Society donated £500 to this very worthy cause.

An interesting and peculiar donation was of £100 to St James' Church in Old Town Poole to assist with the restoration of a 1857 Bates chamber organ in the church's west gallery in order to introduce new educational and community outreach events.

The Society of Dorset Men gave a total of £3,800 to Dorset good causes during 2011/12.

Other charities supported and worthy of mention are Poole Sailability, which gives opportunity to disabled people to experience sailing (£250), and the children's hospice charity, Julia's House (£500). Each year the Society donates to the Dorset Echo Toy Appeal.

In 2013 the Society carried on its tradition of giving generously to Dorset based good causes and the first donation, of £500, was to the West Dorset Women's Refuge.

In the future The Society of Dorset Men will continue and strive to support many more worthy Dorset Charities.

Vice Chairman Andrew Prowse [right] presents the cheque to Molly Rennie, Chairman of the West Dorset Womens' Refuge. Photograph by Michel Hooper-Immins.

Plain or Fancy?

Horrocks & Webb

35 Salisbury Street, Blandford Forum, Dorset.
Tel: 01258 452618
www.horrocksandwebb.co.uk

Sven Berlin of Gaunts

Allan Cooper reflects on the last years of his artist friend - near Wimborne

Sven Berlin in his garden at Gaunts

SVEN died aged 88 leaving two sons and a daughter, Greta.

Greta sculpted "a boy on a skate board". I was rather late for the ceremony close to Wimborne Library. "You have missed the refreshments!" said Greta.

Boy on a skate board" by Greta Berlin

When I arranged an exhibition of crafts and paintings in Wimborne St. Giles Church, Sven let me borrow a large self-portrait. It is a bright picture done in primary colours.

I explored Sven's garden at Gaunts. Several sculptures were dotted about. He showed me a full-size effigy of the Madonna and Child. It had been indoors in a college in Poole; but someone had scratched it. Sven was angry and had it brought home to his shed. Sven hoped that Salisbury Cathedral of St. Mary might display it. Some critics did not like the Madonna wearing a crown. It pleased Sven when I described St. Mary as Queen of Heaven. My old school was St. Mary's College in Southampton.

When Sven died his life was celebrated in Wimborne Minster. During the service, pictures and manuscripts were displayed. They are stored in the Minster.

My last photo of Sven was taken in Wimborne with the Minster in the background. He was wearing a beret.

Sven Berlin wrote a note to the writer from Gaunts in 1986. "Thank you, Allan: Your mastery of the camera amazes me. I entirely agree about the Madonna and Child. Salisbury is where it should be, along with my contemporaries Frink and Hepworth, making a statement from within. Thank you also for your appreciation. SVEN"

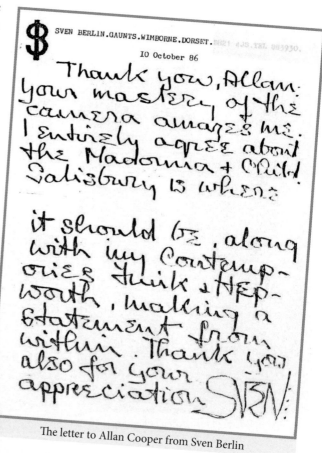

The letter to Allan Cooper from Sven Berlin

BIOGRAPHICAL NOTE: SVEN BERLIN (1911 - 1999) was a British painter, sculptor, poet, writer and dancer. He rubbed shoulders with many twentieth century greats from Robert Graves and Augustus John to Barbara Hepworth and Ben Nicholson. He was part of the Penwith Society of Arts before becoming an adoptive gypsy, travelling from Cornwall to the New Forest by horse drawn caravan. He was fascinated by the Romany culture and wildlife and made an extensive study of fish. After a period on the Isle of Wight he moved to the Wimborne area in 1975 where he remained prolific in painting, writing and sculpture until his death at the end of 1999.

Anyone with a comprehensive knowledge of this British "Bohemian", particularly in relation to his Dorset & Hampshire years, is invited by the Editor to write a feature, with illustrations, on his extraordinary life - for the 2015 Dorset Year Book.

EROS – "the Angel of Christian Charity" – in Piccadilly Circus

the controversy over Lord Shaftesbury's Memorial by Allan Cooper BA FRSA

EIGHT years after the body of Anthony Ashley Cooper, KG, 7th Earl of Shaftesbury, had been placed in the crypt of Wimborne St. Giles Parish Church his memorial in Piccadilly Circus was unveiled, on 29th June 1893, by the Duke of Westminster. Its designer was not present. By the following morning only two of the eight chained drinking cups were left.

The beautiful memorial and its designer, like the good man it commemorated, were targets for both extreme admiration and cruel contempt.

The Daily Telegraph claimed the memorial to be "among the finest the metropolis possesses." A Society magazine insisted that "the naked figure of Love was indecent, and the whole thing ugly and pretentious". A **Times** correspondent – Edmund Gosse – suggested that the naked figure should be placed "over the entrance to the Oxford Street Music Hall or, better still, melted down."

Alfred Gilbert R.A., the designer of the memorial had been doomed to disappointment from start to finish. The commission was for £3000 but it cost him nearer £7,000 owing to a rise in the price of copper.

Wimborne St. Giles' folk totally unperturbed

The Dorset villagers of Wimborne St. Giles – a hundred miles west of Piccadilly – seemed to have been unaware of the controversy that raged in London. The parish magazines for 1893 carried no reports of all the fuss. Readers were told of the two thousand year-old yew tree in the churchyard, of the 9th Earl providing a house for the Village Club, and they followed closely the work of the Day and Sunday Schools and the Penny Bank. In the Summer there were reports of village cricket matches and the flower show. Mr. Brock's peas, it was claimed, were grown from some seed taken out of an Egyptian mummy. Autumn passed with mentions of a choir outing to Bournemouth, and of "bat trap and ball" played at a Mothers' Meeting. Harvest Festival was praised for its decorations and music. Salisbury Infirmary was given half the offertory of £13 2s 9d. Girls were exhorted to bath twice a week. "Flannel next to the skin, loose stays and warm socks will keep many a sorrow from the home, and many a girl from the streets." Real religion came as much from "looking after the drains and careful cooking as in the reading of good books." Mrs. Frances Lockyer died aged 93. The 7th Earl's memorial trust awarded prizes to the best boys and girls in work and behaviour at School.

Interfering committee men, councillors and council officers

It is ironic that so much scorn was heaped upon Alfred Gilbert. The Shaftesbury Memorial Committee at first chose Joseph Edgar Boehm, R.A., to design the memorial. Being too busy, he turned down the invitation and recommended 32 year-old Gilbert, his former pupil.

Gilbert made it clear at once that he was not prepared to put up a "coat and trousers" statue; rather he would symbolize Shaftesbury's life's work. He chose the figure of Love (Christian Charity) to surmount a large bronze base. The site was not one he favoured. Its irregular shape did not inspire him. "An impossible site" he declared, "except possibly for an underground lavatory".

The angel of Christian Charity – EROS – in Piccadilly Circus by Michael Reeve / Wikimedia Commons

Meanwhile the opening of Shaftesbury Avenue and the unveiling of Boehm's statue of Shaftesbury in Westminster Abbey, 1886, and the approval of the design for Shaftesbury Theatre in 1887, all escaped the attention of sniping critics.

Gilbert's studio, on the other hand, was invaded from time to time by anxious and interfering committee men and councillors with council officers. Demands for modifications to the memorial's base and surround, attended by much bickering, thoroughly upset Gilbert. Restrictions on the size of the base caused fountain water to fall on the surface of the road on windy days. The drinking fountains were another suggestion that Gilbert had not planned. They were included at two levels in order to refresh man and beast. It was not unusual to find the customary Piccadilly flower sellers sheltering under umbrellas and poor hooligans were causing pandemonium by chasing loudly round and round and squirting water from their mouths at each other.

The third magnetic pole

Even though the memorial has always been overshadowed by nearby buildings, the life-sized Eros (actually a statue of his brother, Anteros, the Greek God of orderly, lawful love and shared tenderness) has survived the storms that raged round it. Only the building of the underground railway and the outbreak of war have caused its temporary removal. The figure of Love, like Lord Shaftesbury before it, "triumphs over its own repulsions that it may help and raise."

"The darling of London town" can probably claim to be the first large-scale aluminium casting, hollow except for a supporting leg, set up as a work of art. Hyde Park was suggested as a perfect setting and might have stifled much controversy. Even so, W. Macqueen-Pope probably sums up the sentiment that will ensure that the memorial remains in Piccadilly Circus. Asking visitors why they were attracted to it, he was told time after time that "This is the centre of all things, you know." "The place is Magic", he said, "and like London it has a habit of enduring".

People with time to spare can find W.E. Gladstone's wording for the inscription in which he extols Shaftesbury as "a blessing to his people", especially to the deprived class who were soon to be seen round the memorial.

When the Circus underwent reconstruction work in the late 1980s, the entire fountain was moved from the centre of the junction at the beginning of Shaftesbury Avenue to its present position at the south-western corner. It still stands thirty-six feet above the clamour of Piccadilly; "the third magnetic pole", "blindfold love" soaring onwards, symbolizing Lord Shaftesbury's works, and swiftly sending forth his missile of kindness.

. . . .

"You are Lobby Lud and I Claim My 10/-"

---

memories of a 1950s Weymouth seaside holiday by Terry Herbert

NOW there's a character! Lobby Lud was invented to increase the circulation of various National Newspapers. Anonymous employees of the newspaper visited seaside resorts and the Paper printed details of the town, a description of "Lobby Lud" and a pass phrase.

Alan Wheatley played a Lobby Lud figure in the 1947 film of Graham Greene's Brighton Rock.

It was pure guess work as no-one really knew what he looked like but, for some reason, my dad was often approached when strolling along the prom; knotted hanky wrapped around his head and trousers rolled up around his knees. He wasn't amused yet my mum and I would get a good laugh about it.

I never caught Lobby Lud but My Old Man, who was anywhere for a green apple, thought he had "cracked it!" as the following poem suggests.

> I saw ol' Lobby Lud you know, heading for the pier.
> I asked me mum if I could go. She said, "You stay right here".
> Dad had left his deck chair like a bullet from a gun
> Lobby had a ten bob note for each and every one.
>
> The ol' man tore along the beach like something out of hell
> I thought I'd follow on because I might get one as well
> But then alas disaster struck, me dad had stubbed his toe
> Yet how he came to lose his trunks, I guess I'll never know.
>
> Not a very pretty sight, hanky round his head
> Trunks around his ankles and face a crimson red.
> Mum came running with a towel and wrapped it round our dad
> "My God!" she said "just look at you, you must be raving mad."

> Yet dad limped on regardless and made it to the pier.
> On return he looked at me and clipped me round the ear.
> His toe was red but luckily there wasn't any blood
> Nor an crispy ten bob notes, it wasn't Lobby Lud.

The holidays I spent in Weymouth were probably the happiest days of my life. For nearly five decades in my native London, never a day went by without the desire to breathe in the sea air and marvel at those wonderful views across the bay. I now reside permanently in Dorset.

. . . .

Coroner Knows Best

a bit of rustic nonsense by Hayne Russell

PICTURE if you will a Coroner's Court held in a Dorset village some years ago...

The witness who found the body was asked by the Coroner, "How did you find the deceased ?"

To which he was given the reply. "I run roun' ver the p'liceman, an 'ee cut en down."

"Gentlemen of the jury," summed up the Coroner, " It appears to me this is a simple case of felo-de-se." (suicide) "You may now put your heads together and decide on your verdict."

The Foreman turned towards his fellow jurymen and said, "Well chaps, this be a vunny t'do I must zay. Coroner zaid 'ee vell in the zea but wold Benjy zaid 'ee vound en hangen t' a beam.

Well Coroner knows mwore 'bout it than we zo if 'em zaid 'ee vell en the zea us cain't goo agean whet 'ee zaid." To which they all agreed.

"Well Gentlemen" said the Coroner, "Have you reached a verdict ?"

"Well Gentlemen" said the Coroner, "Have you reached a verdict ?"

"Yes Zur", said the Foreman.

"Well, what is it ?"

"Vound drown'd" said the Foreman.

William Barnes and "the Hearing of the Word"

the Dorset dialect is a pure and ancient language,
writes The Rev. Dr. John Travell

I have been given a copy of Professor Tom Burton's book: William Barnes's Dialect Poems: A Pronunciation Guide. Knowing nothing about the science of phonetics, what impressed me on reading this book was a realisation that William Barnes deserves to be recognised as much more than simply the Victorian clergyman and schoolmaster who wrote poems in a Dorset dialect which are difficult for non-Dorset folk to read and understand.

The Sound of
William Barnes's Dialect Poems

1. Poems of Rural Life in the Dorset Dialect,
first collection (1844)

by T. L. Burton

Tom Burton's book - the cover showing
John Constable's 1825/26 painting
of "Mill at Gillingham, Dorset".

What is evident from Burton's book is that Barnes' determination to record for posterity the dialect speech of his native Dorset was the major pre-occupation of his life, and was much more than mere nostalgia for the past. It belongs with his successful efforts to preserve Maumbury Rings and the Poundbury camp from the destructive threat of the new railway being driven through them, which also led to the setting up of the Dorset County Museum in Dorchester.

Barnes, no less than Hardy, was responding to the enormous changes taking place in his society; with the industrial revolution and the invention of the railways. The old patterns of life were breaking up as people moved from the countryside to the towns and, in so doing, changed their customs and their way of speaking. Barnes regarded the Dorset Dialect as a pure and ancient language, with its own grammar, which ought not to be lost. It should be preserved and protected from the increasing uniformity of accent and the changes of vocabulary, as words derived from Latin and French – which were assumed to be socially superior – were taking over from the simpler language of the old Anglo-Saxon.

Such was the quality of Barnes' scholarship that he quickly became internationally known. Burton's book makes it clear that William Barnes has an international reputation as an early and important pioneer in the whole study of phonetics. Burton's bibliography lists books by linguistic scholars in Germany, France, America and Holland, all referring to Barnes. Modern scholars are continuing to study Barnes and use him as a source for the reproduction of the sound of dialect in phonetics.

When I read Burton's book I approached it as an historian, more interested in where Barnes comes in the history of linguistics than in the technology of phonetics. Burton is concentrating on using his knowledge of phonetics to arrive at as accurate an account of Barnes' dialect speech as may be possible. He is not writing a history and therefore does not attempt to place Barnes in his historical context.

It seems to me that what phonetics is trying to do, and finding it very difficult, is to do for words what musical notation has done for music: to create symbols that accurately convey, to those who understand them, the precise sound of the letter or word they represent. People were making music long before any system for writing it down was invented, which meant that to learn a song it had to be heard being sung. Now, through the use of the symbols of notes written on a stave, musicians can reproduce exactly the way that each sound is meant to be heard. Phonologists are striving to create a system of symbols for words so that those who learn them can also reproduce the exact sounds that they are meant to convey.

At the beginning of his book Burton quotes from Barnes' *An Outline of English Speech-Craft*: "Speech was shapen of the breath-sounds of speakers, for the ears of hearers, and not from the speech-tokens (letters) in books, for men's eyes."

Words were meant to be heard before they were ever able to be understood by looking at written symbols on a page. And in writing his dialect poems Barnes wanted them to be read aloud, and to be heard, as we heard them, in the sounds of the authentic Dorset dialect speakers of his time. This was, of course, long before modern technology made it possible for sounds to be recorded – and Burton, in his book, has included a CD of himself reading some of Barnes' poems, in the way he thinks that Barnes meant them to be heard.

English – polyglot speech

A particular problem with English, and the reason why all attempts to simplify how English words are spelt always fail, is because English is a polyglot speech. It is a mixture of words from several different languages; basically a form of old German, using words derived from French, Latin, Greek, Arabic and Indian. It is the meaning of the words that gives their spelling, not their sound.

Medicine uses Greek words like psychology and psychosis, science gives Latin names to flowers and plants. At one time, in order to be accepted as a student at a university you were required to have had some classical education for if you knew Greek or Latin – and French for diplomacy and law, and German for theology and philosophy – you could readily understand the meaning of words simply by looking at the way they were spelt.

This is why English spelling is so complicated, and why you cannot simply spell words to indicate only the way they sound when spoken.

In 1844 Barnes published his *Poems of Rural Life.* Burton says that: "The importance of this collection can hardly be over emphasised. After nearly ten years of publishing poems in dialect using a range of different spelling conventions in attempting to convey the sound of the dialect, Barnes had settled on a spelling system with which he was comfortable."

The way that English words are spelt is a very imprecise guide to the way they are meant to sound when they are spoken. The letters 'ough' are pronounced differently in 'thought', 'cough', 'through' and 'bough'. And different speakers from different parts of the country, or the world, will all make them sound different as well.

The Dorchester funeral directors, Grassby and Sons, have been getting international publicity from our Society President, Julian Fellowes, in his popular television series Downton Abbey. Every time there is a family funeral, the Earl of Grantham announces, "We always use Graassby!" rhyming it with 'grass' and 'class'. But locally we say GraZZby rhyming it with 'jazz'.

In the 1844 collection, Barnes includes a long preface which explains his system in a *dissertation* (a detailed discourse on a subject especially as submitted for a higher degree in a university). By this Barnes is indicating that he wants this to be recognised as a serious work of scholarship. In this he says "The Dorset dialect is a broad and bold shape of the English language as the Doric was of Greek." He derives it as a pure survival from Anglo-Saxon, and so "it uses many words of Saxon origin for which English substitutes others of Latin, Greek or French derivation." He gives examples of the way Latin words have replaced simple English; so the phrase "I will not be put upon" becomes instead "I will not be imposed upon" from the Latin 'impositum'.

Proper posh people's English

Someone learning to sing will be told how to produce a note physically, by learning how to breathe, and by doing exercises using the lips and the tip of the tongue. In Pygmalion, Professor Higgins teaches the cockney flower girl Eliza to get rid of her accent and to speak proper posh people's English, by using the techniques of elocution which also teaches how the sounds of words are physically produced.

Barnes sets out the physical way the different sounds of words are made as 'close sounds', 'open sounds' and the use of lips, teeth, palate and throat, and 'stronger or weaker, or rougher or smoother, expulsions of the breath'.

Phonologists produce symbols to indicate the different ways the sounds of letters are produced and in 1844 Barnes was discovering and developing the methods and techniques that linguistic phonologists, such as Burton, are still using today.

Dialect studies as a discipline – dialectology – began in the first half of the nineteenth century, when local dialect dictionaries and dialect grammars first appeared in western Europe. In 1825 James Jennings published *Observations on Some of the Dialects of the West of England, particularly Somerset*. Barnes refers to this in his *dissertation*. He notes the way in both Somerset and Dorset the dipthong **oi** is changed to **wi** ; so the word spoil is pronounced spwile.

Barnes own *Grammar and glossary of the Dorset Dialect* was published in 1863 for the Philological Society in Berlin, which indicates that he was internationally known by that time.

Old Came Rectory- one time home of William Barnes. Photo by Peter Pitman

Burton says that "such was his expertise on dialectical matters that Barnes' opinion was sought by the two most prominent researchers of English dialects in the nineteenth century; Prince Louis Lucien Bonaparte (for whom Barnes translated *The Song of Solomon* into the Dorset dialect) and Alexander J Ellis (for whose monumental *On Early English Pronunciation* Barnes contributed the dialectal data for the area around Winterborne Came). Burton says that Ellis' "mighty work" was almost a century ahead of his time, "since there was no universally accepted phonetic script, he invented a phonetic alphabet of his own. In fact, he invented two..." Ellis was in correspondence with Barnes who had sent him examples of his own script. Burton quotes: "the late Rev. W. Barnes, Winterborne Came, well known through his Dorset poems, took great pains with a comparative specimen which he wrote in a systematic orthography....and kindly explained by correspondence." Burton includes as an appendix Barnes' contribution to Ellis which includes the poem *Why John has no doubts*, printed in phonetic script.

Barnes' influence in the 20th and 21st centuries

Barnes influence on students of dialect pronunciation has continued since his death in 1886. In 1921 Kurt Urlau had published in Berlin a dissertation on *The Speech of the Dorsetshire Dialect Speakers of William Barnes.* On a visit to Dorset in 1913, to record and listen to the speech of the living dialect speakers, he met Thomas Hardy who confessed that he could speak only imperfectly the dialect that he used so extensively in his works, but trusted that he had a sound knowledge of its vocabulary. Hardy recommended him to meet Harry Pouncy, a well known lecturer on Dorset and a dialect speaker, who, according to Barnes' son, "was the only person who could read his father's works correctly."

Another German, Bertil Widen, had published in Lund in 1949 *Studies on the Dorset Dialect.* Widen came to Dorset in 1938 and 1939 and again in 1946, spending time in the villages of Hilton and Melcombe Bingham because he felt they were free from outside influences, having no railway or industry other than farming. He spoke to farm labourers and rural workers who, when he first met them, were all between the ages of 66 and 72 and had been born when Barnes was still alive.

Just three years after Widen's work, Willis D Jacobs produced *William Barnes, Linguist* – published by the University of New Mexico Press in 1952. Burton gives details of further linguistic studies of Barnes which include *A Survey of English Dialects* published by Leeds University in 1962; a French doctorate *William Barnes, Linguist and Poet* published by Amiens University in 1981 and *The Language and Craft of William Barnes, English Poet and Philologist* produced in 2002 by the Edwin Mellen Press of New York. Burton's works, published by the University of Adelaide Press, must also be added to the list.

FREE on-line book and recordings of Barnes' poems

Professor Burton's own book of 2010 *William Barnes's Dialect Poems: A Pronunciation Guide* now has a companion volume *The Sound of William Barnes's Dialect Poems [Poems of Rural Life in the Dorset Dialect, first collection (1844)]* a recent publication in which Burton explains that, only in an ideal world of scholarship would the 2010 book with its CD of 18 poems do the intended job of readers being able to work out for themselves, by listening and reading, the pronunciation of any of Barnes' poems. He continues, "The only safe way to ensure that Barnes' dialect poems will be appreciated by succeeding generations in the pronunciation he intended for them is to publish a phonemic transcript of each individual poem, and to back up the written record with an audio recording that gives voice to the sounds noted in the written record."

The series, when complete, sets out to provide a transcript and audio recording of each poem in Barnes' three collections of *Poems of Rural Life.* Burton writes " The individual volumes in the series are not critical editions: They do not contain variant readings from different versions of the poems or detail notes on matters of linguistic, literary, social, historical, or biographical interest. The aim is simply to provide a self-contained, uncluttered, and reader-friendly text, which may be read on-screen or on the page, with marginal glosses for any words or phrases that might cause difficulty, together with recordings that may be freely audited online."

This all shows that Barnes continues to be a subject of international interest to linguistic scholars. Only recently Hayne Russell, our Society Secretary, received a letter from Daniel Ross, a linguistics student at the University of Illinois, enquiring about the special features of the phraseology and pronunciation of the Dorset dialect.

Tom Burton is an Emeritus Professor in the Discipline of English and Creative Writing at the University of Adelaide, where he taught for nearly forty years. He has spoken on Barnes at several international conferences and at more than two dozen universities in the UK, USA and Australia, and has put on readings from Barnes' poems at four Adelaide Fringe Festivals.

Free audio files of Burton reading the poems and the book, as a free fully-searchable PDF, are available from www.adelaide.edu.au/press

A Life Worth Living

a reflection on the story of Hubert "Bert" Beavis taken mainly from his new autobiography, "The boy down the lane" - by Trevor Vacher-Dean

ONCE upon a time...a local policeman had to be tough, fit, fair and larger than a Hobbit. He was not required to have a degree in embroidery, train-spotting or other equally useful subject, was expected to patrol the streets alone, had to be good with people, enjoy a sense of duty and was trained to handle any situation; from helping a child cross the road to dealing with the most heinous crimes, tragic events and emergencies.

He was, after all, a self-reliant "British Bobby" who naturally commanded the respect and support of the public, as a member of the finest Police Service in the World.

One such policeman, almost now a figure of legend, was Hubert E. Beavis, or "Bert" to his friends and colleagues, who will be 90 next year.

A native of Purbeck but, at various times of his life, from Cranborne, Gillingham, Poole, Sherborne, Shaftesbury and other places in the county, Bert can truly be regarded as a Dorset man. He is, of course, a member of The Society of Dorset Men.

PC167 Constable Hubert Beavis

Not only, but also...

Bert was not only a policeman but saw service and action with the Royal Navy in WWII, mainly in Motor Torpedo Boats, later witnessing the devastation at Hiroshima.

Then, after 29 years as a rural Constable with Dorset Police, he spent four years with the RNLI followed by a further 10 years as Court Usher at Wareham.

He retired to Swanage and has since spent time fishing for mackerel and lobsters from Chapman's Pool and honing his not inconsiderable skill as a talented marine artist, painting mostly in oil on canvas.

Something of a "Just William" as a boy, and from the same era, Bert was born in 1925 the son of the Kingston village blacksmith and his wife, a hardworking, excellent cook and sometimes employed housekeeper who suffered from migraine. His memories of schooling and roaming the Purbecks are remarkable and his escapades and scrapes are stories that by themselves favour the purchase of his book.

He left school at 14 and trained as a motor mechanic. He was taught to drive before he was 16 and contributed to "war work" by driving a three-ton Bedford truck for a logging company.

Motor Torpedo Boat 777 - a 1981 painting by Bert Beavis - now in Dartmouth Museum

While still 17 Bert went to Dorchester and volunteered for the Royal Navy, subsequently did his initial training in Great Malvern and then returned to Dorset having volunteered for service in the Coastal Forces. The shore based training establishment was HMS Attack, on the eastern side of Portland Bill, and a training flotilla in Weymouth, HMS Bee, which included The Pavilion Theatre. After experiencing many adventures, some lucky escapes and inevitable tragedies, in torpedo boats, in which life expectancy was short, Bert made it to VE Day and his 20th birthday. He was no longer a teenager.

Bert was transferred to the Far East on a fleet maintenance ship, docked in Japan only a short distance from Hiroshima. He witnessed the dropping of the world's first atomic bomb and the devastation caused.

A bobby on the beat

After demob Bert found himself in limbo so, on the advice of a local policeman, decided to try and join the Dorset Constabulary. This was the start of a career that spanned nearly three decades and took him to many parts of the county where he continued to lead an interesting life of incident, apprehension, excitement and humour, mainly as a "rural copper".

After a probationary period pounding the streets of Poole he was posted to Sherborne and over the next few years did stints in Shaftesbury, Gillingham and back to Poole in 'civvies' with the CID, meanwhile meeting, courting and marrying a nurse from Salisbury Infirmary.

In 1955 Cranborne became Bert's patch. He and his wife moved into the old Victorian Police Station and he bought himself a sturdy bicycle to patrol his area, which included the villages of Edmonsham and Alderholt. For ten years Bert dealt with the country folk of Cranborne, from young offenders to the local gentry, and even Royalty.

Shaftesbury was his next deployment; foot patrol in the town, a section car for rural districts and another spell in CID. All sorts of incidents filled his time there, including dealing with a gunman, arsonists and an axeman. For Bert "life was great in Shaftesbury" but so it must have been in all his other postings, judging from his book which is filled with anecdotes; many serious, some hilarious and all interesting to read.

More chapters in Bert's life

Bert decided to retire in 1977 and, true to form, felt he needed to keep busy so joined the RNLI in Poole. He already owned a boat at Chapman's Pool and a house in Swanage. A variety of duties, from setting up exhibitions to ferrying lifeboats to and from stations along the south coast and beyond, gave Bert several years of useful and happy employment until an old injury forced him into retirement... but not for long.

In 1981 Bert Beavis became Court Usher at Wareham Magistrates' Court and brought his many years of experience as a policeman to assist and ensure the smooth running of proceedings. For 10 years he was responsible for and looked after the building; two court rooms, retiring

Bert as Wareham Court Usher in 1988

rooms, public waiting areas, Solicitor's offices and the probation office. He became an approachable face of the law for all involved parties and was asked to stay on when he reached retiring age at 65. He resisted and says that the dramatically changing attitudes to the Police and Judicial System in the Courts, lack of respect from the public and the interference of "European Courts" persuaded him that "enough was enough".

Retirement gave Bert the opportunity of expanding his passion for messing about on his boat and tales of fishing trips off the Dorset coast abound. Although acknowledged as a talented artist in the 1950s, he now had time to indulge in painting, mainly sea scenes. Two, of St. Peter Port lifeboat rescues, hang in The Cornet Museum on Guernsey and Swanage, Poole and Dartmouth are among other museums and galleries to own Bert Beavis' paintings.

Hubert Beavis, now 88 years old, continues to live with his wife Gillian in Swanage. His book, quite aptly, ends with the statement that Bert is a proud member of The Society of Dorset Men, which promotes good fellowship among Dorset Men wherever they may be, and fosters a love of Dorset, and pride in its history and traditions. I, and I am sure my fellow Dorsets, will drink to that! to Bert! and to the success of his book.

The Boy Down The Lane by Hubert E Beavis, 176 pages with over 40 illustrations, retails at £9.99 + £2.50 p&p from Jill Blanchard's New and Secondhand Books, Station Road, Swanage, Peter Crocker, Clay Pitts, School Road, Gillingham, Dorset, SP8 4QR tel: 01747822173 or on Amazon. ISBN 978-0-9553779-6-9.

. . . .

THE OLD PROPERTY LAWS OF BRYANSTON

Freehold or Leasehold? Not likely! Falling under the ancient form of *Grand Serjeantry*, where instead of fighting in wars the recipient held land in return for performing specific duties for the King, *(Brienston)* Bryanston near Blandford was held on the grounds that the tenant should supply a man to carry out a very odd assignment. For 40 days he had to go before the army, when the King made war on Scotland and/or Wales, bareheaded and barefoot, in his shirt and linen drawers, holding a bow in one hand and an arrow without feathers in the other.

That can't have been pleasant for the peasant!

. . . .

Warmest thanks and appreciation are expressed to all who have supported the production of this Year Book and for the co-operation of Contributors, particularly those whose submissions were unable to be included. Every care has been exercised to ensure the appropriate acknowledgement of articles, poetry and illustrations has been given to copyright holders. If omission has inadvertently occurred, apologies are tendered with a request for the owner's kind and courteous indulgence. - *Editor*

Dorset Blue Vinny

Michel Hooper-Immins takes a look at his favourite cheese

DORSET Blue Vinny has a long and mostly unchronicled history. Produced for centuries by farmers seeking a use for spare milk, there are apocryphal stories about musty horse tack, old boots and mouldy breadcrumbs being used to create the unpredictable blue mould. The truth is uncertain- the Public Health Inspector was certainly not as active in days of yore!

At a *Southern Television* recording in Puddletown in the mid Sixties, featuring the late Jack Hargreaves in the popular country magazine programme *Out of Town*, a local farmer in a smock wandered round offering cubes of his Dorset Blue Vinny. I found it hard, dry and rather sharp- harsh and unpleasant. He told me damp hessian sacks were used to introduce the natural mould, covering the cheeses in a corner of a barn. It was sold to local people who called at the farm, but he had not managed to interest any shops. No farmers' markets in those days!

Dorset Blue Vinny wins prizes everywhere-here at the influential Bath & West Show.

There is no doubt the generally poor quality, variable availability and lack of retail outlets led to the scattered production dying out by the early 1970s. Some unscrupulous traders took to passing off second grade Stilton to unknowing tourists as Dorset Blue Vinny.

Dorset Blue Vinny would have remained history, but for the enterprise and enthusiasm of dairy farmer Mike Davies, who took over Woodbridge Farm at Stock Gaylard in 1970, between Sherborne and Sturminster Newton, in the beautiful Blackmore Vale. "Stock" is an Old English word meaning heavily wooded.

The surplus 'milk-lake' to the rescue

Mike Davies, born at Walton-on-Thames in Surrey, is an adopted son of Dorset, having moved to the Blackmore Vale 51 years ago. Studying at Somerset Agricultural College and keen to get into farming, he had started on the bottom rung as a cowman. A course in cheesemaking proved to be useful in later years!

By 1984, just before the quota system was introduced, there was a worrying "milk lake" and prices plunged. Wondering what other use could be made of his surplus milk, Mike Davies remembered that cheesemaking course and Dorset Blue Vinny having died out, he courageously set out to revive the iconic county cheese as a quality product.

He researched the recipe and started experimenting by making the cheese in small moulds- often sliced drainpipes! Every Saturday morning, he would take twenty gallons of milk and disappear to the garage, where his experimental cheese plant had been installed. "Mike's in the Cheese Room" was the cry from the family, as he spent many months perfecting the technique and recipe- "a bit hit and miss at first," he remembers. "Vinny," by the way, comes from the Old English "vinew" meaning blue veining.

The cheeses were then placed in the farmhouse pantry to ripen. Christine Davies was not best pleased. The smell in the pantry was overwhelming and everything around the cheese turned blue! "I received notice to quit the pantry from my wife," laughs Mike Davies, who realised at that point that production had to be on a more commercial basis.

A cow stall was converted and success soon followed. "I knew there was a market for quality Dorset Blue Vinny," Mike recalls. "I sold it first to the Dairy Maid shop in Sherborne and they just couldn't get enough. I was lucky, the market was there, I was able to fill it." So Dorset Blue Vinny was relaunched in a blaze of publicity in 1984- 30 years ago.

Family involvement

Mike's son Richard looks after the 220 resident Friesians, who produce the morning milk, left to stand in a stainless steel vat for a couple of hours, before being hand-skimmed to reduce the fat content to about 3%. "It traditionally was only about 1.8%, but with so little fat in the milk, there was not enough for the spores to work with," explains Mike Davies. "A slightly higher fat content makes a softer cheese, much more suited to modern tastes." Starter is added to the vat of unpasteurised milk, then vegetarian rennet and liquid penicillin spores for blueing.

Once the milk has solidified, it's cut into pieces- now called the curd- and left overnight. The next morning, whey is drained off and the curds cut into small pieces, salted and packed into moulds. For five days, they stay in the warm dairy to encourage the blue veining. After five days, they are taken out of the moulds, then moved to the adjacent Ripening Room, cool and damp, for anything from three to five months.

The longer the cheese matures, the stronger flavour it will develop. All 1,500 cheeses, weighing around 13 pounds each, have to be turned by one of the staff every day. After a month, the cheeses are pierced with stainless steel rods, so the blue vein can develop and spread through. Some may be pierced a couple more times, but development of the veins is rather unpredictable and needs watching. The cheesemakers do the day-to-day work, although Mike Davies keeps a loving eye on his ripening cheeses. That's where his 30 years experience comes in. The smell in the Ripening Room is absolutely intoxicating- as 1,500 cheeses slowly mature, giving off a mouthwatering aroma.

Dorset Blue Vinny is a rare "appellation controlee" in cheese terms, recognised by the European Union as a PGI [Protected Geographical Indicator,] so that it can only be made in Dorset and to the prescribed recipe. Only 14 UK cheeses are protected in this way and Dorset Blue Vinny holds the only PGI exclusively in Dorset.

Emily Davies at the Sturminster Newton Cheese Fair, showing off not only the Dorset Blue Vinny, but the soups and chutneys too. Photograph by Michel Hooper-Immins.

Mike's daughter Emily helps to manage the enterprise, born at Woodbridge Farm and becoming involved in Dorset Blue Vinny from a very early age. Studying business

The dairy farmer who rescued Dorset Blue Vinny 30 years ago- Mike Davies and his daughter Emily. Photograph by Michel Hooper-Immins.

& finance at Winchester Agricultural College, she moved to Lord Mountbatten's Broadlands Estate at Romsey as Farm Secretary. A change of career led to teaching tennis at local schools and Sherborne Tennis Club, but in 2000 she moved back to the family business.

Bubbly Emily is best known as the public face of Dorset Blue Vinny, selling the quality county cheese to the grateful public at Farmers' Markets all over Dorset and Somerset, as well as events like the Dorset County Show and the Sturminster Newton Cheese Fair.

The idea of making soup came into Emily's mind after returning from market, as there was always some cheese left over. Making soup would be a good use for it. In October 2000, she made some trial soups. Friends and family raved about the results.

Nine months were spent writing a business plan for the embryo Dorset Blue Soup Co. DEFRA, the old Ministry of Agriculture, awarded a Rural Enterprise Grant to fund 30% of start-up costs. Brother Richard's workshop was requisitioned as the new kitchen and at the end of 2002, production started in earnest.

Forty different flavours of Dorset Blue soup are crafted during the year, the tastebud trapping smells wafting over the Friesians in the yard. Mushroom, Bacon & Dorset Blue Vinny is a popular variety, as is Leek, Potato & Blue and Sweet Potato & Carrot. Each has a delightful individual flavour, not at all dominated by the blue cheese, the smooth taste blending really well on the palate. Fresh vegetables are used in all the soups.

Emily hit on the idea of packing the soup in rigid plastic containers, easier to store and reseal. Pubs, restaurants and caterers can buy them in resealable buckets! Waitrose sell the soup in 14 stores.

For a decade, she has taken the Dorset Blue caravan to the Glastonbury Festival, selling many gallons of soup to discerning festivalgoers, as well as Dorset Blue Vinny ploughmans and toasties into the night.

"There's a lot of competition in the soup market," Emily Davies tells me, "but sales are holding up and we're absolutely delighted to be in some Waitrose supermarkets."

Then there are Emily's amazing chutneys. My own favourite is the luscious Woodbridge Chutney, a delicious blend of pear and spices. You may prefer the spiced tomato chutney or the sweet pickled cucumbers. Again, Waitrose sell the chutneys in ten stores, as do many Dorset delis.

Today, Dorset Blue Vinny is a creamy quality cheese, consistent and with a growing niche market. On their farm in the idyllic Blackmore Vale, the Davies family lovingly make and tend up to 1,500 cheeses, until they are ready to be sold. Another Ripening Room is being built, which will store 600 more cheeses as production is stepped up.

Thanks to Mark Woodhouse, many Hall & Woodhouse pubs now buy the cheese to offer on their menu in some form- in salads, as sauces and on a cheeseboard. I recently enjoyed amazing braised beef in Dorset Blue Vinny, cooked by Jerry Matthews at the Portland Heights Hotel.

Some cheese is exported, some to the United States and even to London! It's sold at Fortnum & Mason and all good independent delis should stock it.

This extraordinary enterprise provides employment in a rural area, six on the soup & chutney side and three on the cheesemaking. "We have the most amazing versatile team," says Emily Davies, "we all work and laugh so well together."

The smell in the Ripening Room is absolutely intoxicating- as 1,500 cheeses slowly mature, giving off a mouthwatering aroma. Photograph by Michel Hooper-Immins

A Society tradition

Mike Davies meets The Queen in Sherborne last year. Photograph by Emily Davies.

Dorset Blue Vinny is highlighted in the annual ritual at every County Dinner of The Society of Dorset Men, as the cheese is paraded through the room, much in the way the Scots venerate the haggis. Presented to the President to taste, it is subsequently served to all 350 diners with Dorset Knobs and Dorset watercress as the fourth course.

The tradition comes from the early days of the Society, 110 years ago, when Dorset Men in London viewed the annual appearance of their cheese as a tangible link with the home county. "I am so pleased this tradition continues," says Mike Davies, "and feel very proud my cheese is part of such a grand event."

The venerable Pensioners of the Chelsea Hospital are sent a cheese every Christmas for their celebrations- a tradition that started many decades ago.

Some supermarkets sell "Blue Vinney-" note the "e-" produced somewhere in Leicestershire, although some customers may be fooled into thinking it is the authentic Dorset product. Given the omission of the word "Dorset," they are just on the right side of the law as the European Union's PGI includes the county name.

Mike Davies reflects on his 30 years as the creator of modern Dorset Blue Vinny and is delighted the experiment he started in 1984 has been so successful. "I would do it all over again if I had the chance," he tells me, "I think if I hadn't revived it, then no-one else would have done. We have moved with the times, no-one thought of selling online ten years ago. Now we sell a lot through our website- www.dorsetblue.co.uk"

"We still meet our faithful customers at the Farmers' Markets and other outside events. We are diversifying with Dorset Blue Vinny chocolate made by Andy & Clare Burnet at Chococo in Swanage and with Dorset Blue Vinny ice cream by Purbeck."

Mike Davies has no plans to retire and still brims with as much enthusiasm for his cheese as he did 30 years ago.

Perhaps the highlight of the three decades came last year, when Mike met HM The Queen outside Sherborne Abbey on her Diamond Jubilee visit to Dorset. "The Queen talked to me for several minutes," enthuses Mike Davies, "she was fascinated that Dorset Blue Vinny is made from unpasteurised milk and wished us continued success."

I have known the workaholic Davies family for many years and proud to call them friends. The delightful creamy cheese produced by the family is so much better than the rough poor quality cheese I tasted in Puddletown some 45 years ago. I wish Mike, Christine, Emily and Richard many more happy years producing my favourite cheese. Now which of Emily's chutneys shall I have with my Dorset Blue Vinny tonight.....

· ·

CHRISTMAS DAY IN PRISON
200 YEARS AGO

On Christmas Day, the prisoners in Newgate, Ludgate and the two Compters, amounting together to upwards of 900, were ordered each to receive - one pound of beef – one pint of porter – and half a three-penny loaf. Ten chaldrons* of coal were also distributed among them by order of the Right Honorable The Lord Mayor. The Sheriffs have ordered a like donation on New-Year's Day.

Lady's Magazine – 1814

* A chaldron is an old unit of capacity, equal to 36 heaped bushels or twenty-five-and-a-half cwt (approx.1.3 metric tonnes) - **The Editor.**

"The Fulfilled Believer": Jack Clemo in Dorset

by Luke Thompson

Theodore Francis Powys with
Jack Clemo at Mappowder

JACK Clemo was a Cornish-born poet, story writer, novelist, theologian and autobiographer. Among his best known works are the novel Wilding Graft (1948), the autobiographies Confession of a Rebel (1949) and Marriage of a Rebel (1980), and the poetry collections The Map of Clay (1961) and Cactus on Carmel (1967). He was famously deaf and blind for much of his adult life, the last ten years of which were spent in Weymouth.

Jack Clemo first visited Dorset in August 1950 to meet T.F. Powys at his home in Mappowder. A mutual friend of the two writers, Monica Hutchings, had arranged the trip and drove Jack and his mother to the Powys Lodge. The Clemos had travelled up from their lifelong home in the clay mining district of mid-Cornwall. Jack was deaf by this point, and his eyesight was poor. In just a few years his eyesight would deteriorate to a white blindness. In 1950 Jack could still read, but the landscape they were driving through was blurred, so that EvelineClemo and Monica Hutchings had to pass him notes describing the villages and countryside of two of his greatest literary influences, Thomas Hardy and Theodore Powys. Jack subsequently wrote up his own account, in the poem 'Daybreak in Dorset' and in a short essay, 'Pilgrimage to Mappowder', published in *Recollections of The Powys Brothers*. In his diary Clemo called this visit 'the incredible dream-come-true', a 'unique, unforgettable journey'. The story of that visit is itself an interesting one, and not altogether as Clemo wrote it up later, though that story is for another time. For now I'd like to give an impression of the extraordinary spiritual significance of

Dorset for Clemo, the context of his move there, and the role of the *Dorset Year Book*.

There were many reasons for Jack to consider his meeting with Powys fatefully portentous. Clemo was of a superstitiously religious type, in the sense that he did not see coincidences in his life, or accidents, but patterns created by God or conjured by the Devil. And, as Clemo stated as early as 1937 in a local press controversy: 'Suffering any evil, the workings of "coincidence", the rhythms of change – these are revelations of God, and should be studied'. Also, of course, Jack was just starting out on his career, with a single novel and an autobiography

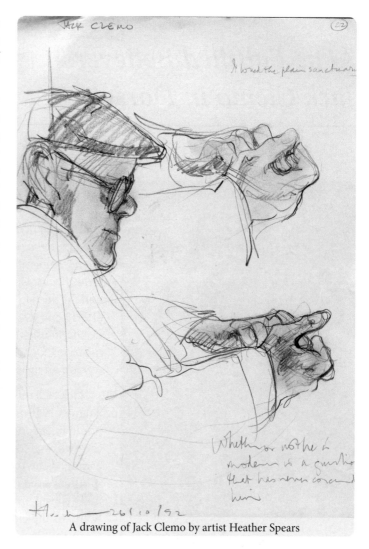
A drawing of Jack Clemo by artist Heather Spears

published, and here at Mappowder was his great hero telling him the work was good and showing friendship. His encouragement of Clemo was taken very intimately, and the temptation to look to the older Powys in a paternal way proved too powerful. As soon as they arrived Powys met them and Hutchings took a photograph of the two writers, which Clemo described as 'Theodore and I holding hands like father and son', before the older writer took his visitors inside, still leading Clemo by the hand, 'so warm and fatherly'. Jack had lost his own father in the First World War, when his ship hit mines in the North Sea and Jack was still an infant.

Dorset – a place of destiny

For the Cornish novelist and poet, Dorset was a place of destiny, a place of meaningful, divinely directed circumstances. To begin with, as already noted, two of the greatest influences on Clemo's prose were Dorset writers, Powys and Hardy. While writing his first novel, *Wilding Graft,* Clemo was immersed in Hardy's work, particularly enthralled with *The Return of the Native*. In his autobiography, *Confession of a Rebel*, he tries to distance his own work from Hardy's a little, implying that he had been writing books like this long before he had come across Hardy's work. However, in his diaries for the years when he was writing *Wilding Graft* the influence is explicitly stated, and it may well be argued that it is only in this novel that any great similarity is observed.

In the second published novel, *The Shadowed Bed* (1986), the influence of Powys is overwhelming, with *The Left Leg* and *Mr Weston's Good Wine* said to have been of particular use. Clemo's novel is a Christian allegory set in the clay region over a single weekend, with the devil being represented as the claywork owner Beale, and God by a farmer named Potter.

(There was a third novel published of Clemo's writing, produced posthumously; *The Clay-Kiln*, a 'cut and shut' job welding together several failed early drafts of novels to make one, which itself was not accepted while the author was alive. The novel was reworked in several decades so its influences are more diverse.)

In a list compiled in 1941, by which time all three novels were either completed or underway, three novelists are among Clemo's list of 'the elect'. These are the two Dorset influences, Hardy and Powys, along with the author of *The Forsyte Saga,* John Galsworthy. The language we read here, of 'election' and 'destiny', are again significant. They are not used as theological theories, but as alive and immediate statements about the world, the result of his being born and raised in a Methodist tradition.

Clemo wrote of 'destiny' in his day-to-day life a great deal, and it is relevant to his receptiveness to Dorset links. It was an 'hour of destiny' when he sent off copies of his first novel to a girl he admired in 1948. Specific dates were observed as 'days of destiny', and 1945, he had calculated, was to be a 'year of destiny'. In the end nothing very special in his personal life happened in 1945 and Clemo was bitterly disappointed, so at the end of the year, over Christmas and into January, he thought again, declaring that 1946 'must and shall be the year of Destiny' instead.

It is easy to mock this pattern-seeking prognostication. A great many times he expresses absolute certainty and faith in something 'destined' to occur, and almost always the happening fails to arrive on time. But the events Clemo looks for are poignant. He is looking for healing, for relief from the deafness and eye trouble; he is looking for a wife, for spiritual companionship and help for when his mother dies.

And he was attentive to his literary destiny. Clemo's work was intended as testimony, so it had to be in the hands of God too.

But also destiny to Clemo could not be something that happened while you did nothing. You did not sit back and wait for destiny to enter you or wash over you. It was something you observed and pursued within God's will. A kind of meeting point to which both you and God were heading. He observed signs and dates, and similarities between himself and other writers that would lend a clue to God's intention for him. Most closely, he observed the pattern of the relationship between Elizabeth Barrett and Robert Browning, an observation that would later become relevant to his relationship with Dorset. This he called 'The Browning pattern', observing the anniversaries of their birthdays, letters, meeting days, wedding days.

So, because of the Hardy and Powys link Clemo was attentive to signs from Dorset, and within the 'Browning pattern' he was expecting to find a like-minded wife.

Jack and Ruth

His joy might then be imagined when he received correspondence from Miss Ruth Peaty, a Christian woman living in Weymouth and also eager for a Christian marriage, in a letter dated 12th September 1967 - the wedding anniversary of Elizabeth Barrett and Robert Browning. This 'coincidence' could not be ignored and within a year Ruth and Jack were married and Ruth had moved to Cornwall, living with the poet and his ageing mother, who had raised and supported her son alone for around fifty years. It would not be for sixteen more years that the Clemos finally moved to Dorset. They spoke about the possibility many times, but did not commit finally until 1984. Before they had met Clemo had already written several poems about his Dorset connections, but now they became as prominent as his Cornish landscapes, with placed pieces like 'Weymouth', 'Isle of Slingers', 'Mappowder Revisited', 'Sandsfoot Castle Gardens', and 'Chesil Beach'. These poems used a new set of symbols of satisfaction, like the Weymouth palm trees, which 'my wife set me writing about'.

Opinion has been divided concerning who really wanted to move, Jack or Ruth, and they were both sensitive to the criticism that Ruth might have coerced him from his birthplace. She had always found the small granite clay-worker's cottage bleak and lonely and she was at heart a town or city girl, born in East London and settled in Weymouth. In a letter to a student writing his thesis on Clemo, Jack noted that 'Ruth did not find it easy to adjust herself to the slow monotonous routine of a lonely cottage in an industrial area.' Ruth was not comfortable in Cornwall, but she was still anxious about moving Jack to Weymouth. They did not know where they had the most friends, nor where would be best for promoting Jack's work, and, of course, Ruth was afraid for her husband's health. In 1980 Jack notes: 'R. is wavering again, afraid we can't cope with the upheaval.' And when they finally did move, it was Ruth who missed it. 'R.

still misses Cornwall much more than I do', he wrote late in 1984, for 'its big shopping centres and cultural stimulus.'

Earlier that same year the couple had spent a last holiday in Weymouth, at the end of which they began to dread the return to Goonamarris, and when they got back, 'The cottage seemed dead – no mail awaiting us in the doorbag, and the TV wouldn't work.' They were ready to move.

Central to this sense of the cottage's 'death', and central to the move itself, was the death of Jack's mother in 1977. Jack and Eveline had lived together all of his life until her death, bearing together the strains of poverty and Jack's sickness. The landscape changed for him once she was gone: 'I did not so much feel that my mother had become dead to me as that the Cornwall she represented had gone dead', he wrote in *The Marriage of a Rebel*, published in 1980. In one way this was literally true. By the time of his mother's death Clemo had been effectively deaf for forty years and blind for more than twenty, so he relied on his mother not only to care for him, but also to translate the world around; news, gossip, village life, and so on. She wrote on his palm, explaining the conversations around them and describing their environment. When she died, so did the landscape of their unusual discourse, and from then on Ruth interpreted the world.

From Cornwall to Dorset

Ruth's interpretation provided the sensory substance for all of Clemo's impressively imageful poetry that appeared through the eighties and nineties. The accuracy and insightfulness of this period's work are exemplified in the Italian poems. Clemo had never seen Italy himself, but was taken there twice by Father Benedict Ramsden, from which trips the two latest collections *Approach to Murano* (1993) and *The Cured Arno* (1995) were inspired. These poems are very vivid, and Ramsden noted that they were full of observations that he, with unimpaired sight and hearing, could not recall. So extraordinary did he consider this that he went back to visit the same places again, and found that his friend had been astonishingly perceptive. All of these visual and audial sensations had been pressed into the palm of his hand by Ruth.

At the same time as the move to Weymouth, there were other changes occurring in Clemo's life, not all of them as positive or decisive. The 'publishing situation is desperate' was a constant refrain through these years. *A Different Drummer* had been ready for publication since 1977, though it did not appear until 1986. So really, between this 1977 collection and the next new volume, *Approach to Murano*, was sixteen years. He was not inactive in this time, but his poetic productivity had dropped considerably following the death of his mother, and it concerned him. So through the eighties Clemo returned to old material, publishing a selection of dialect tales written in the 1930s and some verses for children, entitled *The Bouncing Hills,* and submitting *The Shadowed Bed*, the first version of which had been finished in 1938. Jack also agreed to two selections of poetry, Bloodaxe's*Selected Poetry* and Previous Parrot Press's *Clay Cuts*. James Whetter put together *Banner Poems*, from the 'simple descriptive pieces' largely derived from older work and submitted to *The Cornish Banner*. This decade *Wilding Graft* was reissued, as well as new issues of *Confession of a Rebel* and *Marriage of a Rebel*. In terms of publications the 1980s appear the busiest years of Clemo's life, though in fact his output of original material was at its lowest ebb.

Following the success of *Clay Cuts*, with Stan Dobbin's lovely woodcut illustrations and each limited edition signed by poet and artist, Clemo suggested a similar selection using the newer Dorset poems. However, the publisher believed Cornwall was more marketable, with a more loyal resident readership than Dorset and the collection was never made. It may also have been a concern to the publisher that the pain and fierce tension of Clemo's earlier clayscape poems was more popular than his happiness and mystic fulfilment through marriage, a fact unhappily observed by Clemo too.

A Different Drummer proved very difficult to place, his previous publisher Methuen being the first to reject the manuscript in 1977. Nine years and a great many rejections later it was taken by Tabb House, a smaller Cornish press. Jack's diaries show concern for this waning interest in his work, and in the context of this anxiety the loyal support of *The Cornish Banner* and the *Dorset Year Book* grew in significance. *The Banner* showed that he was not being forgotten in Cornwall, while the *Dorset Year Book* proved that interest in his work reached outside of his home county.

The Dorset Year Book poems

The *Dorset Year Book* poems were published between 1980 and 1996 and were included in the final three full Clemo collections, *A Different Drummer* (1986), *Approach to Murano*(1993), and *The Cured Arno* (1995). The first poem to appear was 'Chesil Beach', in 1980, and Clemo submitted each subsequent year until his death in 1994. Even after his death, two poems were discovered clearly intended for the *Year Book* and published in the 1995 and 1996 issues. It is striking that the original versions submitted here were not altered before their collected publications. Aside from rare minor changes, such as 'wild tusk boar' being altered to 'wild tusked boar', where the former is more likely a typographic error, the pieces were untouched for up to nine years. Some of his earlier poems went through many versions and alterations, with significant variants only a few years apart. The cause of this methodological change may well have been his disabilities; it was no longer possible to read a draft and rework it as he had once done.

2014 marks the twentieth anniversary of Jack Clemo's death, and the thirtieth of his move to Dorset. It seems appropriate to mark both occasions with two poems that show the distance he came. 'Christ in the Clay-Pit' was the first poem written of *The Clay Verge* (1951), which was his first collection of poetry. He noted its conception in his diary on the 4th February 1945: 'Wrote an entirely new poem – "Christ in the Clay-pit" – 38 lines – grim but true.'

The second poem reproduced here, 'Quenched', was the last Clemo wrote, composed on the 21st May 1994, two months before he died. He was staying with a friend in Cornwall at the time of composition, from where they visited their old home.

So the two poems were written about the same area of clay country, the first when Clemo was twenty-eight years old and the last when he was seventy-eight. In tone and style they show the great distance travelled from that cramped granite cottage by the clayworks to his new Weymouth wife and Dorset home.

CHRIST IN THE CLAY-PIT

Why should I find Him here
And not in a church, nor yet
Where Nature heaves a breast like Olivet
Against the stars? I peer
Upon His footsteps in this quarried mud;
I see His blood
In rusty stains on pit-props, waggon-frames
Bristling with nails, not leaves. There were no leaves
Upon his chosen Tree,
No parasitic flowering o'er the shames
Of Eden's primal infidelity.
Just splintered wood and nails
Were fairest blossoming for Him Who speaks
Where mica-silt outbreaks
Like water from the side of His own clay
In that strange day

When He was pierced. Here still the earth-face pales
And rends in earthquake roarings of a blast
With tainted rock outcast
While fields and woods lie dreaming yet of peace
'Twixt God and his creation, of release
From potent wrath — a faith that waxes bold
In churches nestling snugly in the fold
Of scented hillsides where mild shadows brood.
The dark and stubborn mood
Of Him Whose feet are bare upon this mire,
And in the furnace fire

Which hardens all the clay that has escaped,
Would not be understood
By worshippers of beauty toned and shaped
To flower or hymn. I know their facile praise
False to the heart of me, which like this pit
Must still be disembowelled of Nature's stain,
And rendered fit
By violent mouldings through the tunnelled ways
Of all He would regain.

QUENCHED

I have returned in fitful spring rain
To the knot of hills that will never untwist
In trick lightning again, as it did while I lived here.
The hill-knot fantasy has been abolished:
Its switches are stiff and unused, ignoring the sunsets.
No current jabs at the clotting shadows
With strange hints of industrial magic.

Tip-flare, pit-spurt, tank-twinkle –
They thrilled me for years, but they have gone.
The hamlet dwellers are dismayed
By the sudden plunge into wartime blackout,
A daily trauma, the final sting
Of failure in trade bargaining.

I'm glad I escaped this blow:
The clay fantasy blazed around my cottage
When I last slept there. I had watched it, drawn
Into a glow of mystery, not costs and markets.
But I avoid the house now:
It's dark night has no message for me.

Luke Thompson is a PhD candidate studying the work and life of Jack Clemo (1916-1994) at the University of Exeter. He is also on the editorial team of The Clearing, *a new magazine for writing of nature and place.*

The photograph of Clemo with T.F. Powys, as well as the poems and all of the quotes from Clemo's letters and diaries, is used with permission from the University of Exeter's Special Collections Library, where the majority of Clemo's literary and personal papers are held. The drawing of Clemo is by artist Heather Spears, who met the poet in 1992. The image appears courtesy of Luke Thompson.

The Powys Society

a report by Chris Thomas

IN 2013 we commemorated the 50th anniversary of the death of John Cowper Powys which occurred on June 17th, 1963. This was marked by an exhibition at the National Library of Wales in Aberystwyth. The National Library of Wales possesses the largest European public collection of original materials relating to the Powys family; consisting of letters, manuscripts, diaries, drafts of projected works, books, photographs, paintings, and a sculpture bust of John Cowper Powys by the artist Oloff de Wet. Many of these items reveal the close relationship between the Powys family and the county of Dorset and many have been put on public display for the first time. The exhibition remains open until February 8th, 2014. Admission to the exhibition is free.

John Cowper Powys received numerous honours and awards during his lifetime, in recognition of his literary achievements, but the award which must have especially gratified him was honorary life membership of The Society of Dorset Men presented to him in 1962 on the occasion of his 90th birthday on October 8th.

The connection of the Powys family with the county of Dorset goes back to 1837 when JCP's grandfather, the Rev. Littleton Charles Powys (1789-1871), nephew of the 1st Baron Lilford, Senior Fellow and Proctor of Corpus Christi College, Cambridge, was appointed the Rector of Stalbridge. He remained in Stalbridge until his retirement in 1867 when he moved to the nearby village of Henstridge. He later lived with his son, the father of John Cowper Powys, Charles Francis Powys (1843-1923), who was then curate in charge at Bradford Abbas.

Llewelyn Powys's fine account of his grandfather's life as Rector of a small Dorset parish, in *Dorset Essays*, evokes, very poignantly, the long family memory of Stalbridge and its influence on C.F. Powys's children: *"The mere mention of the name of the stately old Dorset market town had the power of stirring my imagination"* said Llewelyn. John Cowper also continued to remember Stalbridge for its name appears in his novels *Ducdame, Wolf Solent, A Glastonbury Romance, Owen Glendower* as well as in his play *Paddock Calls* and in his diaries where he refers to*"the learned and shrewd Rector of Stalbridge"* and recalls *"the smell of old cottages at Stalbridge"*. As late as 1961, in a letter to one of his correspondents, he described Stalbridge as *"a village with a railway station"* (the railway line that linked Glastonbury with Templecomb, Henstridge, Stalbridge, Yeovil, Sherborne and Stuminster Newton was closed later in the 1960s).

Llewelyn Stone

The Powys' contribution to the artistic culture of Dorset

John Cowper must also have been greatly pleased by the honour bestowed on him by the Society of Dorset Men because it implicitly recognised the achievements and contributions made by other members of the Powys family to the artistic culture of Dorset. Gertrude's paintings, Katie's novels and poems, Theodore's stories and fables, Llewelyn's essays, and A.R. Powys's work on the conservation and repair of ancient buildings all celebrate well known, and some less well known, Dorset places, people, and traditions. No doubt John Cowper was kept informed about A.R. Powys's correspondence with Thomas Hardy in 1927 in which he attempted to persuade Hardy to encourage the Society of Dorset Men to acquire Judge Jeffrey's house in Dorchester which was then in need of restoration. Hardy replied to A.R.Powys in a very positive way and agreed that the lodging was *"a most interesting old building and suitable for an annex to the Dorset County Museum."*

The landscape of Dorset features prominently of course in many of his novels, especially in *Wood and Stone, Ducdame, Wolf Solent, Weymouth Sands, Maiden Castle, The Brazen Head* and even in his late space fantasy *All or Nothing.* John Cowper was intimately acquainted with what he called *"this suggestive region"* and could convey, with remarkable acuity and psychic insight, the actual living quality of the orchards, hills, valleys, fields, water meadows, rivers, lanes, ditches, trees and flowers of Dorset, referring, for instance, in *Wolf Solent*, to: "*sap sweet emanations from the leafy recesses of all the Dorset woods*" and to "*lovely breathings from damp moss and cold primroses*".

This was JCP's "Beatific Vision" of Dorset – a place of refuge and secret sequesterment transformed by his creative imagination. The "*umbrageous aura*" of the Dorset landscape which John Cowper loved so profoundly also appeared to him to lead directly to his complex inner self. "*What a country this was...this wonderful country must surely deepen, intensify, enrich his furtive inner life*", he declared in *Wolf Solent*, which must surely count towards a description of JCP's own innermost being. In a letter to his sister, Katie, written in America in 1929 he once described how he sometimes actively called up memories of Dorset as if they were apotropaic images and protective talismans of his inner emotional existence: "*I think of the green seaweed on the wharf steps of the ferry to the Nothe...I think of walking over Lodmoor...I can make the sign of the pentagon round my inner world & can will Iowa, & Georgia, & Michigan & Minnesota into invisibility.*" This sort of protective approach to his private psyche suggests the inner world of Wolf Solent: "*...the core of his being was a little, hard, opaque, round crystal*" which also suggests the goal of Chinese alchemy. John Cowper was well informed about these profound and meaningful things. Many years later whilst still living in America he referred to Dorset when he wanted to describe the weather but without recourse to psychological mechanisms: "*The air has a Dorset tang in it*", he confided to his diary. He continued to identify with his Dorset origins, though he was of course born in Derbyshire, even in old age, explaining to his correspondents the source of one of his favourite phrases "*your wone self*" - "*as we say in Dorset*".

Weymouth – "the centre of my mortal life..."

Of all the places in Dorset loved by the Powys family it was the town of Weymouth and its surrounding countryside that had the greatest influence on the life and writing of John Cowper Powys. Weymouth provided a set of memories of holidays spent at Penn House, in Brunswick Terrace, at the eastern end of the Esplanade, where his paternal grandmother lived and which he describes so well in *Autobiography*. Weymouth's landmarks also provided him with metaphors and images, "*milestones in the landscapes*", that recur frequently in his books like sacred heiroglyphs. No wonder he referred to Weymouth as "*the centre of my mortal life...where I am more at home than anywhere else in the world.*"

Weymouth Sands, the novel he wrote in America between 1932 and 1933, is suffused with a profound sense of "*sea scents and sea murmurs*", of the colour of brittle shells "*on the wet and gleaming Weymouth sands*", seaweed waving to and fro at the bottom of rock pools, and of the Dorset coast with its hinterland of green fields and chalk downs. The novel is also imbued with a perfectly realised sense of physical location and the spirit of place. But the town he describes is strangely immaterial and insubstantial – it is an ideal place constructed out of light and colour, and out of air and water as if he was making an *aquarelle* or watercolour. It was as though he saw everything through the glamour of a "*mythological haze*". The effect is of course quite deliberate.

Weymouth remained for John Cowper a place of childhood vision, where he experienced moments of intense happiness stirred by the sight of sun paths glittering on a shining sea across the pebble bank outside the house of his grandmother, as if this allowed him entrance to another world. In 1961, gathering up his store of memories, he wrote in the preface to a new edition of *Wolf Solent*: "*...Penn House... was the gate to the tides and pebbles and sands of the salt sea.*"

Society 'study day'

John Cowper's novel *Weymouth Sands* was also the subject of our first study day in Ely, Cambridgeshire. Our Chairman, the artist, Timothy Hyman, led a discussion of the novel focussing mainly on Chapter 10, Sea Holly, but which extended also to cover the main themes of the whole novel. He circulated some visual guides to help us find a contemporary context for the novel such as some old postcards, photographs of Weymouth,and a copy of the Ward Lock guide book to Weymouth published in the 1930s. Timothy also showed us a stone from Chesil Beach as well as an example of the sea holly plant and introduced the discussion by explaining the role of the book in his own life – it was the first book he had read by John Cowper which was around the time of the great Bonnard exhibition in London in 1966. He pointed to similarities in the way both John Cowper and Bonnard approached the use of colour and treated their characters and figures.

We discussed the autobiographical facets of the book, how some of the characters are clearly based on real people, recalling that John Cowper himself said he had spread himself over three different characters. We discussed the friendships, affairs and broken relationships in the novel, as well as the weak plot line (which JCP admitted). We also discussed the comic aspects of the novel and the significance of the elements of air, water and stone. Our meeting concluded with a discussion of the transcendent role of Weymouth as a place, embodying both personal memory and redeeming the sense of failure, loss, annihilation and sadness which seems to brood over many of the scenes.

The library at the Dorset County Museum

In June a small group of members of the Powys Society met in the impressive library of the Dorset Natural History and Archaeological Society in the Dorset County Museum to read and discuss selected passages from the writings of the Powyses on the theme of love, friendship and family relationships –real and imagined. A broad selection of texts were chosen representing John Cowper, Llewelyn and Theodore as well as Louis Wilkinson who was a long standing friend of the family. We debated the veracity and reliability of Wilkinson's memoirs of the Powys family recorded in his book *Welsh Ambassadors*, first published in 1936, and discussed the importance of family relationships and love affairs in both the real lives of the Powys family and in their imaginative works.

The library at the Dorset County Museum is indeed an impressive place with its long refectory central table, high ceiling, well lit corners, and tall book lined walls containing over 30.000 volumes and over 1000 bound periodicals , covering subjects such as geology, archaeology, natural history, geography, social history, local history, and the literature, art and architecture of Dorset. The library provides a good resource for research (a dedicated computer terminal in the library now allows free access to JSTOR, which is a powerful on-line academic digital archive containing thousands of scholarly periodical articles) but it can also be used as a comfortable reading room.

"A hollow leading nowhither"

In the afternoon, following our discussion, we were joined by members of the South Dorset Group of the Rambler's Association who accompanied us to the village of East Chaldon (called in the Domesday Book Chalvedone) where we embarked on a circular walk from the centre of the village, to Chydyok farmhouse, once home of Llewelyn, his wife Alyse Gregory, Katie and Gertrude Powys, located high up on the expansive chalk downs, and returning on rough flint and chalk paths via West Chaldon, where

Chydyok

the strong fragrance of wild herbs was very noticeable. The weather was perfect – a clear, cloudless azure blue sky allowed views all along the cliff top as far as the White Nose and shimmering in the distance we could see the outline of Portland. Above us the gulls cried and screamed wildly.

The area here is full of interest – we stopped to read passages from books by the Powyses and explore the garden of Chydyok farmhouse with the remains of the wooden hut, where Llewelyn rested and John Cowper read to him from *Paradise Lost*. We studied Llewelyn's memorial stone, placed south of Chydyok in the corner of a field in 1947, examined the strange sculptured stone whelk shells tucked inside boundary walls on the cliff top, and looked at the monuments in the churchyard of East Chaldon.

Sir Frederick Treves in his book, *Highways and Byways of Dorset*, published in 1906, called East Chaldon "*a hollow leading nowhither*" and "*a long forgotten village*. Despite the attraction of The Sailor's Return and the presence of a trail of holiday makers and literary tourists, looking for traces of Sylvia Townsend Warner, Valentine Ackland and Theodore Powys, the village still feels like a place hidden by secluded combs and chalk valleys.

Annual conference

The Powys Society annual conference entitled, "*Placing John Cowper Powys*", was held at The Hand Hotel in Llangollen on 16th to 17th August. Over 40 members participated and a lively, friendly atmosphere and a strong sense of Powysian community spirit was much enjoyed by everyone. The annual conference is a good opportunity to greet new members, meet old acquaintances, share our joint enthusiasm for the writings of the Powys family and exchange ideas, views and opinions about their work.

Conference speakers included our President, Glen Cavaliero, poet, Fellow Commoner of St Catherine's College, Cambridge and member of the Royal Society of Literature, who opened the conference, gave us a lesson in practical criticism and presented an informal talk on the pleasures of reading the Powyses; Katherine Saunders-Nash, Assistant Professor of English at Virginia Commonwealth University, USA, who presented a lecture on the serpentine quality of John Cowper's novels; Charles Lock, editor of the *Powys Journal*, discussed contemporary modern European literary links with John Cowper's novel *Wolf Solent* as well as its local and regional characteristics; and Robert Caserio, Professor of English at Pennsylvania State University, USA, who discussed JCP's *Autobiography* in the context of other English and American autobiographies of the 1930s.

A guided walk to nearby Corwen and a visit to John Cowper's home for over twenty years, at Cae Coed, was followed later by an entertaining reading of two of Theodore Powys's *Fables,* presented by our Newsletter editor, Kate Kavanagh, and past Chairman, John Hodgson, and an open discussion with members.

President - Glen Cavaliero and Hon. Sec. Chris Thomas

A hot topic

Our publications this year have included three *Newsletters*, Volume XXIII of the *Powys Journal*, and a new book entitled *Ultimate Things: Christianity, Myth and the Powyses* by W.J. Keith, Emeritus Professor of English at the University of Toronto. The broad range of subjects and original material published in our Newsletters and scholarly Journal testifies to the enormous reservoir of unpublished writings by and about the Powys family still awaiting discovery and continuing research.

Ultimate Things is a very useful synoptic examination of the differing attitudes to Christianity, mythology and religion by individual members of the Powys family but especially the response to Christian and other religious themes and ideas in the works of John Cowper, Theodore and Llewelyn Powys. The book includes a study of the contemporary context of religious and philosophical debates, the influence on the writing Powys brothers of their father , C.F. Powys, his traditional religious faith and their strongly held independent and sceptical views. This is *"a hot topic"*, as our reviewer of the book in the July Newsletter commented, providing some much needed clarification of the religious ideas of the Powyses and will be of significant interest to anyone studying the inter-relationship between the history of Christianity and literary history in the nineteenth and twentieth centuries.

The Powys Society owns an important collection of original manuscripts, letters, photographs, diaries, sketch books, drafts of unfinished writings, paintings, sculpture, *ex-libris* books (some with significant marginal annotations by the Powyses), as well as rare presentation copies of books, and various other artefacts associated with the Powys family. The core of the Collection was bequeathed to the Powys Society by two private collectors, Mr E.E. Bissell and Francis Feather. We are indebted to our benefactors for their generous gift.

The Powys Society Collection offers a unique opportunity for study, research and access to documents unavailable anywhere else. The annotated catalogue of the Collection can be found on-line on the Powys Society website.

The Collection has been housed in two small rooms on the top floor of the Dorset County Museum in Dorchester for over twenty years. Having now outgrown our storage space, The Powys Society, with the mutual consent of the Trustees of the Dorset Natural History and Archaeological Society, has recently entered into discussions to explore the potential to move the literary parts of the Powys Society Collection to the Special Collections of Exeter University. Exeter University has an outstanding reputation for archival acquisition and management and we are confident the Powys Society Collection will be very well cared for at their repository, where the archives and literary papers of writers with Powys' links, such as Sabine Baring-Gould, Henry Williamson, Jack Clemo, A. L. Rowse, G Wilson Knight, Patricia Beer, Daphne du Maurier, Eden Phillpotts, and John Fowles are housed.

We will of course continue to maintain our much valued links with the Dorset County Museum where the Writer's Gallery will maintain the permanent display of Powys family exhibits. In the meantime the Powys Society Collection can still be accessed at its present location at the Dorset County Museum on application to the Collection Manager, Michael Kowalewski, whose contact details can be found on the Powys Society website.

Our events program for 2014 is still in the planning stages but we expect to hold at least two study days, one of which will be at the Dorset County Museum in Dorchester in June and we expect our annual conference will be held in Sherborne on the 15th to 17th August at the Sherborne Hotel.

If you would like to find out more about our activities, or join the Powys Society, please visit our web site at: www.powys-society.org , contact Hon.Secretary by e-mail at: chris.d.thomas@hotmail.co.uk or write to Chris Thomas, Hon. Secretary, The Powys Society, Flat D, 87 Ledbury Road, London W11 2AG.

The Powys Society is a registered charity (801332). It was founded in 1967 with the aim of promoting public education and recognition of the writings, thought and contribution to the arts of the Powys family, particularly John Cowper, Theodore and Llewelyn. The Society is international, attracts scholars and general readers from around the world and welcomes anyone interested in learning more about this very talented and unusual family.

A Moment in Time?

a trawl back through my area's history by Dave Allan

I want to tell the story of Weymouth and district from the perspective of a 21st Century tourist. Easy? Well, no ! – but taking time over a cup-of-tea and a slice of local Dorset apple-cake, in Hope Square, helped me ponder the conundrum. In a flash it came to me!

It's my job – I'm an historical guide

A visitor came and asked for directions to the Information Centre. "I'm afraid it's gone," I said, "Council cutbacks, Olympic Legacy, the economic climate, ……..!"

"I'm looking for the Timewalk and the museum" the stranger asked. I started to explain.....

Sometime later the fascinated tourist asked how I remembered all the facts. I replied with disdain – "It's my job – I'm an historical guide and run the new Heritage Centre

Dave Allan in character as a History Guide

round the corner in the converted 18th Century Sail Loft." ... And so my journey back in time began from this little part of Dorset where we were sitting!

Not so long ago this very street was filled with expectant sports fans on their way to the Olympic viewpoint to watch the 2012 sporting heroes win the greatest haul of medals by British Sailors ever seen – history in the making! But, when viewed from my table, what had gone before?

As the "time machine" inside my brain accelerated into the past, I thought on the heyday of Weymouth in the previous 20th Century; of the "Timewalk Exhibition" now long gone, of the Devenish Brewery and the legacy of Weymouth's past. Images flashed through my thoughts. Just as in the film adaptation of the famous novel "The Time Machine" by H.G. Wells, the story of the Old Harbour began to peel back the layers of time like an onion.

The Second World War, with over 500,000 American Soldiers passing through this very town, and the dark days just 4 years earlier when the Nazi war machine tried to crush this quaint Harbour town under a torrent of bombs.

The depression of the 1930's, the wonderful preceding roaring 20's and before that The Great War, with the arrival of fighting men from Australia and New Zealand – this time wounded in a far off land at Gallipoli, and arriving for medical help in nearby Melcombe Regis. Their legacy now gone, but remembered in the place names around the Westham area of Weymouth, and the Commemorative services held during each year.

Moving faster now, my mind racing back to the Victorian heyday of a vibrant Royal Holiday resort, with the Queen and her German Prince Consort, if only they could have known what was to come after!

As the building at the back of the square was deconstructed, it would reveal a Georgian past, with all the glory of a former Royal resident – another German Royal, this time George III of England, and Hanoverian Elector. The Old Rooms behind my table was "the place" to visit, with the once famous meeting rooms of Delamotte's being the party house of the King's brother and the rest of his extended family. Society tolerating, if not actively supporting, the local Smuggling fraternity who provided those little luxuries of life at "cut-down" prices – with tax avoidance transactions to the rich, and not so rich! A single line from Rudyard Kipling's famous poem "and watch the wall my darling, as the gentlemen ride by" sums up in a sentence the hidden secrets of the local economy supported by those who were of means (and those who were not!)

The local author of the story "Moonfleet" – John Meade-Faulkner - would be writing and telling the story in 1898!

The maritime heritage revealed

Then my little bit of Dorset was suddenly a lot wetter! Not because of the Great Storm and Tsunami of 1824, but because the Old Harbour was pre-1781. The tidal inlet that gave rise to the town's prosperity became a harbour once again. The maritime heritage revealed, the journey now made easier with the passage of ships and small boats passing into the River Wey, and out to the world into Weymouth Bay. From the Smugglers of the 18th Century, back to the Monmouth rebellion, and the terrible retribution of the infamous Judge Jeffries after the defeat of rebels during the 1685 rebellion.

Then the Jacobite legacy of the Stuart Dynasty, with the forgotten battle and siege of Melcombe Regis and capture of Weymouth town by Royalist Soldiers in 1645. The cataclysmic action in and around the harbour in this year helped lead to the execution of a King in 1649 after his last remaining Army is crushed at Naseby.

The area was to witness carnage on a grand scale, now hidden from knowledge in a veil of secrecy drawn over massacre, intrigue, local support and bitter fighting all around my little bit of Dorset!

Racing back in time to a period of Piracy and Privateering, exploration, trade, and the full glory of this little bit of Dorset, and the earlier Royal connection of the Tudor Dynasty, making our town famous with visitors and merchants from around the world, from Newfoundland to India, and from Spain to America.

18th C. Timewalk, Heritage & Visitor Centre

Tudors & Plantagenets

The terrible wars in Europe during the 16th Century, and the part played by Dorset men in the defeat of the Spanish Armada in the waters off Portland, made possible by Elisabeth, Queen of England, and her formation of our Borough in 1571.

Before the Tudors we are visited by the Plantagenets, as Queen Margaret of Anjou lands on our beaches in 1471 in an attempt to regain the throne for her son, Edward, Prince of Wales – a bad day as "Warwick, the Kingmaker" is killed at the Battle of Barnet and the Campaign will end with death, and disaster at Tewkesbury!

My little bit of Dorset has so much to it's past that the local stories flow in and out like the tides that wash these shores – sometimes happy and prosperous, sometimes sad and foreboding as events occur in the paragraphs of history!

Earlier Plantagenet King's both arrive and depart during the Hundred Years War (1337 – 1453) with France, with local ships supporting our Country's attempt to reclaim the lost throne of France.

An unwelcome guest arrives in June 1348 – an unknown visitor from a far off land in the form of the Black Death! The infamous town across the River reputedly being the first casualty in Britain to suffer the fate of thousands from this foreign pestilence.

Just two years earlier the little Ports of Weymouth and Melcombe Regis send the largest contingent of men and ships under Edward III in his bid to capture Calais in 1346/7.

With this we accelerate back to the Norman Conquest and the great castle built overlooking Ope Cove on Portland by William Rufus.

In a flash the Dark Age invasions of Vikings, defeated by the men of Wessex in Dorset. Then Saxon's arriving around 400 years earlier and destroying the far older local Romano-British settlements, and then back to the first Century, with the local Durotriges Tribes destroyed and subjugated by the might of the Roman Empire under General Vespasian in 43AD.

Then we are back in time before Rome, with the Iron Age, Bronze Age, and Stone Age, and even to the Neolithic period when man first settles in the area on Portland – perhaps the first true "Dorset Men"? All of a sudden we are brought back to the 21st Century, sitting at a little table with a stunned visitor.

"Well, if you have time during your stay, pop into the Weymouth Timewalk Heritage & Visitor Centre round the corner on the old Harbour side and I'll enlighten you some more"

And that's the story of Dorset Men. Who's a'feared?

Bunny and Copper and Me at Burton Bradstock

my early years on Manor Farm by Beverly Lenthall – "that was"

Beverly in 1950

WHERE I grew up was a place of 'great goings on!'

John "Martin" Lenthall – "Bunny" to his friends – was not a man to let the grass grow under his feet. Miriam – "Copper" because of her red hair – was his wife and my mother.

When we all arrived at Manor Farm in 1947, Bunny's father, "The Guv'nor", was still very much in charge; to the point that it was Mum who asked if Bunny could borrow the car for the evening and "could he have his wages, please!"

The Guv'nor, a slightly built, quietly charming man with blue kind eyes, was my *mate*. I was three years old and he always called me his little maid. He would walk for miles over the farm, taking me in one hand with his stick in the other, carrying me when I got tired. Smut the black Labrador never leaving his side.

Always smart in tie and jacket with brown gaiters and boots, he did leave me asleep beside the river once. Mum got to hear of it and our walks were stopped for a while! He was very ill and became bedridden. I used to go and sit on his bed while Mum looked after him. He faded away and died in July 1949, three weeks before my sister Susie was born. I remember my Mum crying and crying. She had loved the kind old man who was so gentle with everyone – except his son. They had both hoped that he would live to see the new baby, the first to be born at Manor Farm for many years, but it wasn't to be.

'Copper' with Beverly and Susie

No 'mod-cons' and plenty to do

After Susie came along Mum was even busier. No mod-cons but filthy clothes to be washed in the boiler with a Dolly stick to swish the clothes around, constant visitors to cook for and the dreaded floor to be kept clean.

The old part of the house is a foot below sea level. The kitchen, the office and the *dark hole*, a kind of pantry used for storing preserves and curing bacon, were paved with big grey stone slabs and keeping them clean was a full time job.

Burton Bradstock in 1951

I was left to wander. Smut the dog was a good friend and the imaginatively named cat 'Black and White' went through hell as a surrogate baby in a dolls pram, his patience a legend among cats!

If Dad caught sight of me I'd be given a job. He'd take me around the farm saying "Come on, you can come with me to North Hill." Oh no! It was miles away. "You hang on to the end of my stick and I'll pull you along." I knew it would take hours. North Hill was being cleared of gorse with caterpillar tractors bulldozing the scrub for it to be burned. Then the re-seeding began. This must have been around 1949/50 and I expect there was a government subsidy for encouragement.

At five years old, September 1949, I was sent to the Grove School in Bridport. I caught the bus and walked to the school at the other end on my own. I remember trudging up the drive in my felt hat and massive navy coat which reached almost to my ankles! Bought to last as fashion was for grown-ups only!

Weekends and holidays

At weekends and holidays we kids had to help on the farm. I had to brave a flock of geese who individually were as big as me and used to run at me and hiss when I was sent to get milk from the dairy. We kept a milking herd of Lincoln Reds, crossing them with Hereford bulls for beef cattle.

On one occasion, when I was about five and a half, about 40 dairy cows were out to grass on Port, which meant they had to be driven along Southover and through Burton

Bradstock village, turning in left just after the Three Horseshoes pub. After lunch one day Dad yawned, said he was really tired and jokingly said "Oh! go and get the cows in for me Bev." I took him at his word, walked to Port and rounded them up, hallooing and hollering as I had heard Dad do, waving his stick at the slow coaches. Imagine his, and Mum's, surprise on seeing the cows, and a bull, coming in for milking all on their own. They couldn't see me behind the herd as I was so little.

Spud picking was done for three pence a line; each one seeming to stretch over the curve of the Earth.....and stone picking. The old horse would be hitched up to the *putt*, a small cart, driven to a ploughed field and we kids had to pick up all the stones we could find to put in gateways to make them passable in winter.

I was sent to Burton Mill to ask for the sluice gates to be changed so the water would run down different channels for sheep washing. All the sheep would be thrown in the sheep-wash about two weeks before shearing 500 of them.

Flooding, fishermen's advice and farm wages

If there was a threat of flooding, almost an annual event before the River Board did the flood defences, I'd sit with Dad in the kitchen waiting for the tide to turn. High spring tides and the wind in a certain quarter and we'd be flooded to a depth of four feet all through the house. The water used to ooze up between the floor slabs and up the drains first. The first rush of water would squirt under the doors and around the door frames in jets so powerful that my Mum's new washing machine was ripped out of the electric socket.

The fishermen would come and knock on the back door and either say "You better get the stock out Boss, we've pulled the boats right up, it's looking nasty," or, if we were lucky, "Think the wind is on the change, we've left the boats where they be to, think it'll be alright for now."

Every Friday evening, after work, the farm men would come and wait at the back door for their wages; the two Freds, Sibley and Sealy, Fred and Dave Legg and others, me amongst them. I had to be last...always! As each one was paid, having signed the wages book, he came out, replaced his cap and went home for supper. Then my turn...

Even when I was just able to toddle around, I always went for my wages. Dad would call me in, stand me in front of him as he sat in the boss's chair and asked, "what have you done this week little maid for your wages?" I told him all the jobs I'd done, greatly exaggerating as I got older, and he'd give me a proper wage packet with my name on it.....just like the men.

St. Mary's Church, Piddlehinton captured atmospherically on a winter's day by Andrew Hepburn. Just one of countless examples of the beauties of Dorset's ecclesiastical heritage to be seen throughout the County. The 15th century tower is handsomely decorated and well preserved with its embattled parapet, square vice turret and pinnacles with crocketed finials.

In each wall of the tower is a belfry window from which issued, according to a church notice, a peal of bells rung for four hours and two minutes by Samuel Nelson, Robert Biles, William Old, Timothy Nelson, and Adam Nelson on Christmas Day morning in 1820.

The County "Veast" 2013

by Society of Dorset Men - Hon. Secretary Hayne Russell

OUR President Lord Fellowes took the chair at the County Dinner, which was again held at the George Albert Hotel, Warden Hill, Evershot on Saturday 26th October, accompanied by Lady Emma Fellowes and his guests, The Lord Lieutenant Mrs Valerie Pitt-Rivers, the High Sheriff Mrs Catriona Payne and her husband and the Garrison Commander at Blandford Camp, Colonel Mathew Fensom. Together with 206 members and their guests (a rather disappointing number considering the 330 places available to us), they sat down to an excellent meal which included Dorset Lamb and, of course, the traditional Blue Vinny Cheese, Dorset Knobs and watercress received with the usual ceremony by our President.

The President welcomes his guests to the County Dinner.
[Standing:] His Honour Judge John Beashel DL; John Payne; Colonel Matt Fensom [Commander of the Blandford Army Garrison;] Lord Fellowes of West Stafford DL [President of the Society of Dorset Men;] Colonel John Blashford-Snell OBE; Stuart Adam [Chairman of the Society of Dorset Men.]
[Seated:] Kay Beashel; Catriona Payne [HM High Sheriff of Dorset;] Valerie Pitt-Rivers [HM Lord Lieutenant of Dorset;] Lady Emma Fellowes LVO; Judith Blashford-Snell; Dr. Karola Steidl.
Photograph by Michel Hooper-Immins.

The Challis Cup for the most members recruited was won by the Hon. Secretary Hayne Russell and the Hambro Golf Cup by Mr. Tom Lane.

Our first speaker was His Honour Judge John Beashel who, although now retired from full time bench sittings on the Western Circuit since 2008, is now a member of the Parole Board. He entertained the gathering with some very humorous stories concerning his own experiences whilst a barrister and judge. He proposed the toast "Dorset, our County" having said that he "considers Dorset the best County in England!"

Hayne Russell [Secretary of the Society of Dorset Men] receives the Bryan Challis Cup from Lord Fellowes, for recruiting most new members this year.
Photograph by Michel Hooper-Immins.

He was followed by Colonel John Blashford-Snell OBE who is, of course, a very well known and respected explorer. He described his work in setting up the programme to test the 400 young people who had been selected from an original 50,000 applicants for places on the "Operation Raleigh" initiative. The tests were extremely challenging, varied and sometimes terrifying! However, the experience gained resulted in some caring and professional leaders who later became involved in some very interesting community projects.

Finally, our Chairman proposed the toast to "Our Guests" and paid tribute to the Lord Lieutenant who was in her final year of office. He then proposed the toast to "Our President" thanking him for his continuing support. Lord Fellowes then wound up the very successful evening's proceedings. The toast master Mr Colin Fry had conducted the evening with his usual aplomb and professionalism.

Valerie Pitt-Rivers [HM Lord Lieutenant of Dorset;] Lord Fellowes of West Stafford DL [President of the Society of Dorset Men;] Lady Emma Fellowes LVO.
Photograph by Michel Hooper-Immins.

Articles of interest, humorous or otherwise, prose or poetry, are solicited. All contributions must be voluntary and should be of a "Dorset" flavour. Contributions, with illustrations where possible, will be welcomed by post to the Hon. Editor, Trevor Vacher-Dean, at Rosslyn Cottage, 8 Love Lane, Weymouth – DT4 8JZ or by e-mail to vacherdean@yahoo.co.uk

Please ensure the correct postage is applied to all mail. Stamped addressed envelopes should be sent if mss or 'pictures' are to be returned. The Editor accepts no responsibility in case of loss and reserves the right to edit or condense contributions.

RULES OF THE SOCIETY

(Incorporating the alterations passed at the Special General Meeting of the Society
held on 14th November, 2008)

NAME

1.   The name of the Society shall be "THE SOCIETY OF DORSET MEN."

OBJECTS

2.   The objects of the Society shall be:
      To make and to renew personal friendships and associations, to promote
      good fellowship among Dorset men wherever they may reside, to foster
      love of County and pride in its history and traditions, and to assist by every
      means in its power, natives of Dorset who may stand in need of the influence
      and help of the Society.

MEMBERSHIP

3.   The Society shall consist of a President, Deputy Presidents and Honorary
      Deputy Presidents if desired, Life Members, Vice Presidents and Ordinary
      Members.

QUALIFICATIONS

4.   Any person connected with the County of Dorset by birth, descent, marriage,
      property or past or present residence in the County, shall be eligible to be
      elected to membership.

MODE OF ELECTION AND TERMINATION OF MEMBERSHIP

5. (i)   The names of all candidates for election shall be submitted to the Committee,
          who shall have full power to deal with the same.

   (ii)   The Committee shall have power to remove from the list of Members the
          name of any Member whose subscription is in arrear for 12 months.

   (iii) The Committee may also at any time in their discretion terminate the
          membership of any person without furnishing reasons for their action, in
          which event a pro rata proportion of the subscription will be returned.

SUBSCRIPTIONS

6.   The Subscriptions to the Society shall be:

   (a)   Life Member - one payment £150.00
   (b)   Vice-President - per annum (payable on the 1st October) £15.00

(c)   Ordinary Member- per annum (payable on the 1st October) . . .£10.00
These subscriptions will apply whether the member is residing in the UK or
overseas.

OFFICERS

7.   The Officers of the Society shall be:
Chairman, Deputy Chairman, Honorary Treasurer, Honorary Editor,
Honorary Secretary, Honorary Membership Secretary and Honorary
Newsletter Editor and they, together with the President and Deputy
Presidents, if desired, shall be elected at the Annual General Meeting each
year.
The Committee shall have the power to fill any vacancy arising during the
year.

COMMITTEE

8. (i)   The Society shall be governed by a Committee not exceeding twenty in
number, to be elected from the Members at the Annual General Meeting.
In addition, the Officers of the Society shall be ex-officio Members of the
Committee. Seven shall form a quorum.

(ii)   The Committee may delegate any of their powers to a Sub-Committee.

(iii)   The Committee shall retire annually, but shall be eligible for re-election.

(iv)   Not less than twelve days before the Annual General Meeting the Honorary
Secretary shall send to every Member a notice of the Meeting. The Notice
shall also intimate to the Members that any two Members may nominate one
or more Members for election as Officers or to the Committee, and that such
nomination must be sent to the Honorary Secretary not less than four days
before the Meeting.

(v)   The Committee shall have power to fill any vacancy arising during the year.

MEETINGS

9. (i)   The Annual General Meeting will be held on a date to be decided by the
Committee.

(ii)   The Committee may at any time convene a Special General Meeting and they
shall do so within six weeks of the Honorary Secretary receiving a written
requisition signed by not less than twenty Members. Members requiring
such Meeting shall state in their requisition the subject or subjects to be
discussed, and the resolution or resolutions to be submitted thereat.
Notice of the date and place of all Special Meetings shall be sent by the
Honorary Secretary to each Member twelve clear days prior to the date fixed
for the holding of a Meeting, and such notice shall state the object or purpose
for which such Meeting is convened.

BOOKS AND RECORDS TO BE KEPT

10.   Proper Books of Account, showing all receipts and expenditure, shall be kept

by the Honorary Treasurer, and the Honorary Secretary shall record and keep Minutes of all Meetings of the Committee. The Membership Secretary shall record and maintain a list of members.

EXAMINATION OF ACCOUNTS

11. At each Annual General Meeting two Examiners shall be elected to examine the Accounts of the Society for presentation to the members at the next Annual General Meeting.

ALTERATION OF RULES

12. These Rules may be amended, altered, or varied by a majority of two-thirds of the Members voting at a Special General Meeting.

COMMITTEE CHAIRMAN: STUART ADAM

Court Barton, West Bagber, Taunton, TA4 3EQ. Tel: (01823) 432076

Members of Committee:

P. ASHDOWN, G. KING, S. CREGAN, A. PROWSE,
J. ROUSELL, A. HUTCHINGS, S. WOODCOCK

OFFICERS:

Hon. Secretary: H. C. RUSSELL,
34 Brunel Drive, Preston, Weymouth, DT3 6NX. Tel: (01305) 833700
E-mail: hrussell@gotadsl.co.uk

Hon. Assistant and Membership Secretary: P. LUSH
25 Maumbury Square, Dorchester, DT1 1TY. Tel: (01305) 260039
E-mail: peterlush3@hotmail.com

Hon. Treasurer: I. MORTON
1 Wainwright Close, Preston, Weymouth, DT3 6NS. Tel: 01305 832722
E-mail: ianvalmorton@fsmail.net

Hon. Editor "The Dorset Year Book": T. VACHER-DEAN
Rosslyn Cottage, 8 Love Lane, Weymouth, DT4 8JZ. Tel 01305 781261
E-mail: vacherdean@yahoo.co.uk

Hon. Newsletter Editor: M. L. HOOPER-IMMINS,
2 Waverley Court, Radipole, Weymouth, DT3 5EE. Tel: (01305) 779705
Email: hooperimmins@btopenworld.com

Society Archivest and Historian: REV DR J. TRAVELL
44 Cornwall Road, Dorchester, DT1 1RY. Tel: 01305 264681
E-mail: johntravell@outlook.com

IN MEMORIAM

The President and Members mourn the loss of the following worthy
fellow Dorsets and tender their sincere sympathy to their relatives.

KENNETH DODD *(Swanage)*	Ordinary Member	2012
ALAN BAXTER EVANS *(Wimborne)*	Life Member	12.4.2012
DESMONDE SAMSOME *(Wareham)*	Ordinary Member	27.8.2012
KENNETH LEGG *(Swanage)*	Ordinary Member	19.9.2012
COLIN G. HARVEY *(Blandford)*	Overseas Member	4.11.2012
G. R. K. UDELL *(Holt)*	Vice President	17.11.2012
F. EVILL *(Gillingham)*	Ordinary Member	4.12.2012
WILLIAM SHALDERS *(Charlton Marshall)*	Ordinary Member	15.12.2012
ALAN J. QUINTON *(Beaminster)*	Vice President	2013
TERRENCE K. RODDICK *(Studland)*	Ordinary Member	2013
D. W. WINCH *(Ferndown)*	Ordinary Member	2013
JAMES (Jim) CLARE *(Dorchester)*	Vice President	11.1.2013
PETER BOTTERILL Gp Capt CBE AFC *(B'ford)*	Life Member	27.3.2013
RONALD BLANCHARD *(Swanage)*	Ordinary Member	6.4.2013
DAVID BAGGS *(Wareham)*	Vice President	10.4.2013
F. EVILL *(Gillingham)*	Ordinary Member	12.4.2013
PETER HARRIS FCA *(Dorchester)*	Life Member	21.4.2013
MICHAEL GURD *(Bridport)*	Vice President	12.5.2013
REGINALD POND *(Swanage)*	Ordinary Member	20.5.2013
W. H. BATTEN *(Upcerne)*	Life Member	27.5.2013
MERVYN ALLEN GIBBS *(Alton Pancras)*	Ordinary Member	30.5.2013
JOHN F. SANSOM *(Wareham)*	Ordinary Member	6.2013
HOWARD MICHAEL EGAN *(Swanage)*	Ordinary Member	2.6.2013
ALFRED BARRETT *(Dorchester)* (Ex-committee member)	Life Member	16.6.2013
JOHN HOLMES *(Cerne Abbas)*	Ordinary Member	14.7.2013
MICHAEL J. ROSE *(Gillingham)*	Ordinary Member	27.7.2013
COLIN W. LUCAS *(Dorchester)*	Ordinary Member	30.8.2013
JOHN CHEELE *(Dorchester)*	Ordinary Member	15.10.2013